ANGUS DAVITT

AND THE

CONVERGENCE

By: Gregory W. Young

ANGUS DAVITT AND THE CONVERGENCE

by Gregory W. Young

Published by Gregory W. Young 2018
in conjunction with "Createspace.com"

ISBN: 978-1-7323247-0-1

Inquiries should be directed to Publisher's email: gwy1101@aol.com

SOURCES OF INSPIRATION

Jule Spohn- **Newark Memories**

Robert Randolph- **The Boys From New Jersey**

Charley Reese- **545 vs. 300,000,000 people**

Neil Sheehan- **A Bright Shining Lie**

Boy Scout Handbook for Boys, 1965 edition

Lynda Van Devanter- and Christopher Morgan- **Home before morning**

THANK YOU!

Gina, who put up with me locking myself away at odd hours for long periods of time, and who helped in editing and putting together the final manuscript.

My son Christopher, the artist "Original Skullboy", who gave Angus Davitt life.

Dr. Gerald S. Mills, who provided expert critique of the first draft and who has been an amazing spiritual mentor.

Ron Jennings, my well qualified law enforcement guru.

Jilly, the marketing specialist of the family who handled production and media.

Sarah Jacobs, Jacobs Design & Print for book layout and cover work with Skullboy.

The "Manly Men", the reason I did this.

My oldest and dearest friends from school days, John and Tommy.

Any and all who served in Vietnam, any and all who serve in the arm forces today for America, and all law enforcement. Without the rule of law and those who defend it, no democracy can survive.

INTRODUCTION

I thought long and hard about whether I would write this book. Writing is not my profession. I did write "The High Cost of Dying", a consumer guide to the funeral industry published by Prometheus Publications in 1995. It received excellent reviews and is still in many libraries. I know the effort it takes to write anything worthwhile.

I have lived a long and blessed life. My family had become tiny, just my son Christopher and me. Then I met my life partner and soulmate Gina. When I got her I got a great family as well. In 2016 Chris and I, Gina's son, her brother and his two sons and her son-in-law drove a motor home from Jersey to Florida for the "Bourbon and Cigar Fueled Manly Men's Retreat" accompanied by "Buddy" the bulldog.

We ranged in age from 15 to 70. In deference to the youngest Manly Man there was not much debauchery. In fact, this diverse group spent much time engaged in philosophical, political and religious debating while we cooked and spent the evenings in my home.

I found myself filling in historical background about things they were not familiar with. When the looks on their faces became particularly puzzled they would ask for more detail and I would backtrack and fill in with more information to add to their understanding. I have not had a quiet life and found myself telling stories about my life when I was their age. Somewhere in the midst of this someone said, "I think you should write a book."

So I began to think about it and once I started I couldn't stop. They were growing up in the world they inherited from me. Did they know how much different our lives as young men were from theirs? It is difficult to know where you are if you don't know how you got here. Did they know anything of life without social media and political correctness? Did they know what the inner city riots and Vietnam did to us?

This book is really a historical crime novel in the form of a memoir. The public events and public persons are as accurate as I can make them. There was much research because the historical accuracy of the events that shaped today's United States is essential. Feel free to fact check. The locations exist/existed. Yes, every experience in the first section of the book happened to me in one form or another though they may have been modified to fit the plot. The second part of the book, "The Convergence" has the Narrator doing things with which I am intimately familiar. The accounts of offshore powerboat racing are as accurate as I can make them. I am an APBA 2 time North American Champion in my class. I raced in 4 World Championships.

DISCLAIMER: "Shoretown" does not, nor has it ever existed. It is my attempt to create a microcosm of the flavor of all Jersey shore towns rolled into one. All characters, other than the public figures, are creations of my imagination. They were created to depict the life we lived during that time period. Any resemblance to anyone living or dead is sheer coincidence. The exceptions are Annie and Dr. Gerry Mills who gave me permission to use their names.

ANGUS DAVITT AND THE CONVERGENCE

Prologue

1990

Police Sergeant Angus Davitt was trying to figure out what the hell was going on. A minute ago he was booking a drunk. Now he was face first against the wall, spread eagle, relieved of his weapon and held by two patrolmen. He had been frisked and his pockets turned inside out. Chief Farquar shouldn't have been there on this typical Saturday night, but he was. Angus caught bits of the confused conversation Chief Farquar was having with the drunk.

"Where's the money?"
"It's not on him, Chief."
"Well, find it!"

The night had started as a typical Saturday night in Shoretown. Angus was in command of the shift with 4 patrolmen on the street and another sergeant with him at headquarters. The whole department numbered only 30. Saturdays were high on drunks and low on crime. Angus followed the usual routine as he collected the next drunk from the holding cell and took him to the booking room. He had to wake up this particular middle aged guy, disheveled and stinking of beer. Angus half walked and half carried him to the booking room. He got him into a chair on one side of the table and began the inventory of the drunk's personal affects. Cheap watch, one chain that could have been gold but probably wasn't, one set of car keys and a wallet with no money in it. The property sheet filled out by the arresting patrolman said there should have been $560. The drunk had his head down again apparently asleep.

"See you for a minute Sergeant?", came from the duty patrolman outside. Angus no more than reached the hall when he saw the Chief and two other cops who were not on his shift. Now here he was up against the wall trying to put the pieces together. The drunk was suddenly very sober and Angus realized this was a set up. The Chief and drunk exited the room and headed for him, money in hand.

"Found it under the table" said the drunk who Angus now understood was a plant. The Chief was in a tough spot. The drunk's job had been to plant the money on Angus but it never made his pocket. Bad timing. The drunk, a private investigator from up north, had been in the process of putting it in Angus' pocket when they called Angus out. Farquar had tried to take Angus down and it had gone bad. Now what? No choice, improvise.

"So you saw me and dumped the money right? No time to write up a new property sheet so you dumped it." said Farquar.

"No matter. For now you're charged with mishandling property. You're on administrative leave as of right now. Leave the belt and the duty revolver. Any back up on you"?

Davitt removed the .38 Detective Special from the ankle holster and handed it over. They escorted him out and he went into the night alternating between being furious and confused.

"WHY?"

Most of Angus Davitt's family were on the Elizabeth, New Jersey Fire Department. Irish immigrants passed through Ellis Island in the 1800's and either ended up in New York City or across the Hudson in Jersey. Many arrived during the Civil War and went straight into the Union Army. Angus' grandfather had arrived later and missed the conflict. He did what immigrants to this country have always done. He broke his back to make something of himself and passed on the work ethic to the next two generations. He settled into a house in Elmora, the Irish section of town. Three generations of Davitts lived in that house at one time. Angus did what he had to do as a kid in a house that needed money. He was running numbers from the corner drug store while he was still in grammar school. In his later years Angus' father would go on about how the community loved to play the numbers. That was until the State took it over and made private numbers illegal. The odds were better when numbers was private.

The Irish had found their niche in American society. Being a cop in New York or fireman in New Jersey provided a nice income and a secure future. One hand washes the other. They got their job through town hall and provided a solid voting block for the politicians that put them there. Angus grew up rawboned, strong, could haul hose like a mule and was fearless. Angus became a fireman the week after he left high school. He made it a few years before boredom set in. His whole future was laid out for him and he never had to go 5 miles from home.

In spite of the fact the Jersey shore was less than 50 miles from New York, it was still country by the sea in the 1950's. Shoretown was less than 4,000 people in 26 square miles bisected by rivers leading from the pines to the sea. Indians were using the banks of the rivers as a summer camp as late as 1900. Then the State built the Garden State Parkway. City was brought to the town. The day they opened The Parkway south Jersey became a day trip from the NY/NJ metropolitan area. Angus' uncle had moved there and opened an auto repair shop before the Parkway. He managed to get himself elected to the town council. Prior to the Parkway the State Police handled law enforcement. Now massive growth dictated the town establish a police department. Opportunity often isn't what you know but who you know. Thanks to his uncle, Angus became badge #9.

Angus lived the cop life 24/7. He made sergeant a few years later and was now up for lieutenant as the department tripled in size. He met Sally in the Clerk's office. Her family was from Elizabeth. He remembered them but couldn't remember her. Now he couldn't forget her anytime they were apart. A few years younger, her disposition was as fiery as her red hair. He met his match and so he married her.

Now it had all gone to hell. The crap didn't get any clearer when the town formally charged him administratively with mishandling property and kept it from becoming a criminal matter. Losing was not in Angus' nature, but Sally worked in town hall and the change in attitude toward her made the work in the clerk's office miserable. He took a job driving a delivery truck, unable to find anything else because he was branded a crooked cop. The case dragged on until he took the deal they offered him. There was no reason to stay. He had 20 years in and so did Sally. Between the buyout they gave Sally and the deal they cut with him, Davitt would be okay They rented their house which had been paid off the previous year, piled their stuff into a Volkswagon van and headed for the Florida Keys. That is where I met Angus Davitt, on the abandoned old bridge at Boca Grande on the way out of Key West, netting shrimp riding the outgoing tide into the Straights of Florida.

West Orange

You can clearly see where the whole thing started from New York City. Look west across the Hudson River from any tall building south of 42nd Street. The planes take off and land at Newark Liberty Airport as they did when we were kids in the 1950's. Beyond, is Newark itself and then East Orange and Orange. The coastal flat land ends abruptly where Orange meets West Orange at the base of the low mountain range. We were born into those mountains in 1946-1947. These are the same mountains on top of which George Washington's scouts kept an eye on the British who had driven them out of New York. When I was a child the world revolved around me. Those mountains served as a barrier dividing my perfect little utopia from any parallel universe and insulating me and my crew in our suburban neighborhood. The back side of these hills are still heavily wooded thanks to being preserved as park land. We knew it as the "reservation" and it was our playground. My house was on one side of Northfield Road and the reservation was on the other. After school we dumped our bags and went outside. If there was no school we seldom finished breakfast before heading out. There were two rules: The first was get home before dark. We raced the sun and made sure we did. A grounding and having to stay inside was the worst possible punishment. The second rule was to not cross Northfield Road so we didn't, we went under it. You see there was this drain pipe about 4 feet high that ran under the road between the creek where we overturned water rounded stones to catch crayfish and Turtle Back Rock. The rock had a geological pattern that gave it it's name. We could sit on top, fifty feet over the road and watch the cars go under our feet. I took my son there when he was 8 and showed him all this. I showed him the tree that was our elevator to the ground. Three feet from the cliff, only a foot around and with smooth bark, we could jump to it and shinny down. When I showed it to him the elevator was gone, too big to put my arms around.

Our parents issued us air rifles that shot nothing but air and had a recoil. It took us a couple of minutes to figure out we could plug the barrel with mud and shoot each other with the plugs. When we got home our mothers were there or if they weren't we simply went to our friend's house and his mother kept us fed. They kept house and our fathers worked. Newark, to the east down the mountain, emptied it's office buildings of our fathers and sent them home in time for dinner. In the fall we raked the fallen leaves against the curb and lit them. We could throw in acorns to hear them explode, we could stand in the smoke or we could leap over the fire.

Carol King wrote a song about West Orange, "Another Pleasant Valley Sunday". Growing up there in the 50's and 60's was like living a scene out of "Happy Days". We were raised by parents who had won WWII. If they fought, they lived through horrors they wanted to forget. If they didn't fight, they found other ways to win the war. My Aunt gave up being a blues singing piano player to assemble bomb sights at Caldwell Airport. My Uncle led the mules carrying ammunition up the mountain at the battle of Monte Cassino in Italy while most of the soldiers pinned down by the Germans at the top kept their heads down. He was never hit. My father was stationed safely in Louisiana. He lost a part of his hand when a captain accidentally discharged a .45 automatic. I never heard any of the other parents talk about the war. The only time my father and his brother talked about their experiences was after Christmas dinner when the bourbon kicked in. War was not nostalgic. War was to be forgotten. West Orange was a product of the generation that won the war. Our parents wanted only peace, a car, a modest house with a bedroom for each kid, and a steady job. They succeeded. We grew up in happy and innocent times. Sure, in grammar school we were taught to dive under our desks if the Russians dropped a bomb on us. One neighbor actually built a bomb shelter. But that was amusing and having the Russians drop a bomb on us was distant to our crew.

I often think of my grandfather. He kept pictures of family in Ohio right after the Civil War. He knew those Civil War veterans when he was a kid. I still have the Civil War rifle he picked up on the family farm. He traveled by horseback and train. Then he went through WWI, WWII, Korea and Vietnam. Curious, I found records of HIS grandfather who settled Cold Stream, Kentucky in 1730 as a pensioner from the French and Indian War. We grew up with a feeling of belonging, tradition, family, and modest success. We were free to adventure and we did. In the 1960's West Orange produced these kids: Ginny Duenkel won a gold and a bronze in swimming in the Tokyo Olympics and they named the town pool after her. There are the two Kelly astronaut twins for whom they just named a school. Retired General Paul Kern is one of the few 4 star generals. There are the two brothers who both had careers with the Secret Service. There was the demur girl who was an operative for the CIA. There are others who achieved great things and if I didn't name them, I apologize.

This book is not about them, the ones who achieved great things. It is about the rest of us and how we ended up in later life. I could not imagine we would be thrown back together decades later. I sit here reflecting on that journey. Maybe this is the normal process of an aging man reviewing a life he lived. Perhaps it is the subconscious desire to revisit simpler times. It could be I am just trying to make sense of it all. None of it comes without some pain and I feel it like it was yesterday. I know one thing for sure; this is not about regret. I am very glad I met Angus Davitt on that bridge in the Florida Keys.

ANOTHER PLEASANT VALLEY SUNDAY
Carol King

1960

We were thirteen. I had spent all but the first two years of my life on this street of middle class homes that were built right after WWII. We walked to school, of course. The neighborhood grammar school was at the end of our street down the steepest road I have ever seen, steeper than anything I saw in San Francisco. We glued ourselves to the radio when the weather got bad in the winter, praying for a "snow day" when school would be closed. The DJ read the list alphabetically. Being West Orange we had plenty of time for the suspense to build.

This particular day it had started to rain during the night. By day break the temperature had dropped 20 degrees in a half hour. Outside my window was the most wondrous natural thing I had ever seen. Every surface was coated with an inch of ice. Trees were breaking under the weight and no one was going anywhere, except for us. I stepped outside and there it was, opportunity. My driveway and the road were sealed under a perfect sheet of pure, clear crystal, smoother than the Zamboni at the skating rink could make, ice.

Karl called me. He and Rocco would meet me where the school path cut down through the woods to the top of my road where the sharp dropping street plummeted into the school grounds. I laced on my skates, pulled on my hockey gloves and careened down the driveway onto the flat street, hung a rink turn to my left and kept up the momentum down the street to where it climbed gradually up toward our rendezvous point. Going up was tough. I zigzagged in order to climb. For Karl and Rocco it was all down hill and they were already there when I arrived. They stared, I stared, no one said anything. Dropping off under the toes of our skates was the smoothest, most perfect ice God had ever created. Our adolescent brains were computing the possibilities for maximizing this experience without actually breaking anything. What an opportunity! Never seen it before, and probably, never see it again.

The road/ski jump track plunged 110 yards. It "T boned" into the street at the bottom, which of course had a curb, on the other side of which was the school grounds. It would be impossible to stop when we hit the bisecting road at the bottom so it was jump the curb. That delivered us onto the mild sleigh riding hill that was probably 50 yards long. The school grounds had a chain link fence on the other side of the sledding hill. We were in perfect synch. No words need be spoken. Rocco went first followed by me. Karl lagged behind to assess what happened to us before he started down.

Within 25 feet we were screaming down that hill. We soon reached terminal velocity at which we passed the point where we could hope to stop. The best we could do was turn across the face to try and maintain control. If we fell we would be picking up speed on our backs or stomachs until we hit the curb. Rocco straightened out at the bottom, timed the jump over the curb perfectly and looked like a triumphant ski jumper as he used the 50 yards of field to scrub off speed before he executed a perfect hockey stop and leaned against the chain link fence. For me, nano seconds became minutes as I felt the pressure on each side of the skate boots, thought ahead to the next turn, planned when to straighten the run for the curb jump and saw that Rocco was clear. Then, disaster. I had never tried to jump a curb on skates at 35 mph. I landed the skates on top, somersaulted forward once, flattened out and spun around on my chest like a helicopter rotor. I don't think I slowed at all before I hit the bottom of the chain link fence in the exact middle between two steel poles. It gave a couple of feet and flung me back to it's original position. Karl came down in perfect control, stopping to pick up my hat first then my right glove ten feet further down, then my left glove while Rocco and I sat and just soaked it all in. We looked at each other still not speaking. Our grins grew into laughter as we felt the adrenaline rush. The sun came out soon after and it only took minutes for the black roads to melt it all. We three brain surgeons walked home in our socks with our skates over our shoulders. Perfect.

We may have invented the game of "Kicking Goals". I came into it already being played so I can't be sure. The flat part of our street had telephone poles equal distance apart. They marked the length of our "field". The curbs marked the sidelines. Anyone who showed up played. The strongest member of one team either passed or kicked the football as far as he could. If the other guys made a clean catch the catcher passed or kicked it back from the spot of the catch. If the ball was dropped, the throwing team moved up to that position and threw again driving the other team back. The battles raged for hours with teams often coming within inches of a goal line before a clean catch in the end zone and a missed catch by the attackers shifted the balance of power.

From behind his bedroom window James watched us play. He was always "James", never "Jim". We liked him. We never understood why he couldn't be out with us after school. What did "going to become a priest" have to do with hanging out with us?

He heard his Mother behind him but did not turn as she spoke.

"Did you finish your homework, dear?"

"Yes, Mother."

"Then start on your catechism, dear."

Yes, he thought, there was always the catechism, always the catechism, always ----------

The northern boundary of our lives was the scout camp that to 13 year old's, was savage and serious. Sarge's Plymouth station wagon stopped at the top of the hill that led over the dam to the camp. The dam held back a man-made lake of crystal water in a deep valley surrounded by the mountain rims of the Appalachian Trail leading from New Jersey into Pennsylvania. The woods were as thick as they had been when the Lenape Indians called it home only a hundred years before. Hikers gazing off the top of the Delaware Water Gap into Pennsylvania wouldn't know the camp was there even though they were only a couple hundred yards above it. Our road, Northfield, became Route 10 as it headed North and West. The drive from the suburbs of Newark to the camp should have taken only a couple of hours on old Route 10. There was an occasional restaurant or gas station 30 miles into the trip but that was about it. Today the drive could take just as long on Interstate 80 when you get caught in the traffic jam of skiers from New York seeking man-made snow and hotels and restaurants in the Poconos. In the 50's and 60's the camp was isolated and might as well have been Alaska. This particular Friday night was not out of the ordinary. The snow had started about half way there and the last part of what should have been a 2 hour trip turned into a 4 hour crawl on a serpentine mountain gravel road rapidly filling with snow. If it had been black top we never would have made it.

To the 7 boys with Sarge it was a right of passage every time we came here. If we made it in, there were no phones and the World War II walkie talkies as big as payphones were only good for talking to each other inside that valley. Even short wave radio would not have escaped over the ridge line. We stayed in uninsulated shacks heated by cast iron pot bellied stoves that glowed cherry when fed. Our water came from a hole chopped in the lake ice. On more than one occasion we were forced to stay an extra day or two during these winter weekends simply because the car couldn't make it out until a county snow plow came down to us. If we didn't have enough fire wood, if we went through the ice, if we got lost in the woods, if we chopped ourselves with an ax or seriously cut ourselves with a knife we were in trouble. Sarge knew the mountains could kill us. To us it was serious play. Later in life I skied Vermont and there were signs on the edge of the ski runs warning, "These woods are as cold and dangerous as they were 200 years ago, stay on the trail!" Been there done that.

During The Great Depression the camp had been constructed by the Civilian Conservation Corps, a government program that put Sarge and thousands of men to work when that was the only way they had food and a roof over their heads. There were no jobs and there was no money, but there were plenty of men who wanted to work. Sarge liked the work. He and the others had first carved the twisted road out of the bottom of the mountain on the side away from the camp. At the start they lived in the town of Stillwater. As the road got longer they shifted their base to the mountain and camped higher until they reached the ridgeline at the top and started down toward the valley that would become a lake. Their carved ribbon of natural gravel reached the stream in 1934. It took them 2 months to construct the cement and boulder dam and spillway and another 2 months to complete the road up the other side into the flat floor of the valley. They felled the pine trees and cleared an area for parking and base buildings. The pine trees went into floors, walls and roofs. Sarge stayed on and joined the forestry service. He got a couple of dollars a day, a roof over his head and plenty of work he loved.

When World War II started Sarge trained at that camp before they shipped him out to Europe. We never knew exactly what training was going on there or exactly what Sarge did during the War. Whenever we asked about the German Luger pistol he carried all the time he was in the woods he only told us that he "got it overseas". When the camp was turned over to the Boy Scouts after WWII they inherited a rifle range and floating docks, base buildings and tent platforms. The Boy Scouts also inherited Sarge.

After he came home Sarge didn't consider family life. At this point he was comfortable as a bachelor. We were his family and each year he brought more boys into his troop, trained them and watched them go off into life. He taught us life skills, how to be men and cut us loose to go on. Pecking orders were established under his watchful eye. The strong rose to the top but he made sure the weaker were nurtured. He brought out the best in everybody, weak or strong. The camp was a microcosm for adolescent male development. Sarge would have made a great psychologist if he had been interested in formal education. He was content as an oil burner repair man.

It was early January and the station wagon's headlights pointed into air at the top of the drop to the dam. The snow blew horizontally picking up speed as it was funneled between the ridges, down the mile long frozen lake and over the top of the dam. Past the front wheels the road dropped to the ice covered dam and back up the other side to the parking lot. The dam was only a hundred feet long and about a lane and a half wide. The lake was right up to the edge on the passenger side. The dam dropped 30 feet into a stream bed on the driver's side, the drop separated from road by an iron pipe rail 3 feet higher than the road bed. Sarge stepped from the car. His foot went through the snow and hit glare ice on the gravel road. He caught himself on the top of the door before he went down.

"O.K. guys that's it, get out and walk down off the side of the road."

"Karl, you're out first."

Karl always rode front seat shotgun. He opened the door and held onto the car, working his way around the rear until he was in the snow and trees on the driver's side. Rocco was next. Karl reached and pulled him into the trees. I was next and we went one after another. "Steinman, are you nuts? It's below zero put your hat and gloves on", said Karl. Sarge smiled but kept it to himself.

We worked our way down the slope from tree to tree and hugged the railing over the dam. The walk up the other side was easier. We gathered in the parking lot standing in snow about six inches deep. We waited for Sarge to pull this one off. He kept his driver door open, car in first gear, foot off the brake and let it roll down the hill. When the road flattened out on top of the dam he hit the gas and blasted up the short hill into the parking lot. He only lost the back end after he crested the top of the hill and so he let the car do a couple of lazy 360's into the center of the lot, pointing back toward the dam. He got a round of applause.

"Karl, you and Fatty make it to the cabin and start a fire. We stay here until you heat it up." Yeah, I was "Fatty". Sarge knew the inside of the cabin was no warmer than outside. The car offered the best shelter until we got some heat inside. I was always the one chosen as the fire starter when it mattered. I could get hot coals using fire by friction with a bow and drill or sparks with flint and steel. The summer I was 14 I experienced the "Vigil". I was told to go to the top of the ridge on the south side of camp as the sun was setting. I was given three matches and a canteen and told to keep a campfire going all night, to not fall asleep and to return at dawn. It was summer but it could get damn cold on that ridge and I was allowed only shorts and a tee shirt. I selected a spot on a big rock as the sun set over the Water Gap and I gathered fire wood in the dark. I used one of the three matches. I stayed warm by the fire and during the night, the leaders who had sent me there, crept in close and I heard voices talking to me from those unseen.

The next morning I carefully extinguished my vigil fire and returned to their handshakes and satisfaction. This was a right of passage appreciated much more in later life.

Night time in a snow storm with 8 people depending on me wasn't play time. I had Sarge's nickel plated Zippo lighter with a raised American flag on it. No messing around, we could freeze to death out here. Karl's job was to get me there. We were cautious watching our footing and made the 100 or so yards in a few minutes. The cabin door was made from tongue and groove pine plank with a cross buck plank holding it all together. The latch was a simple piece of wood that slid down into "U" shaped brackets. When you were on the outside you removed it and when you were on the inside you slid it into the inside brackets. We closed the door and headed for the pot belly stove. Whoever had the cabin before us had done their job. There was plenty of newspaper, kindling and a supply of split dry logs. I had the fire going in less than a minute and fed it ever just larger pieces of wood until I could put on the small logs without snuffing the life out of it. Karl used his light to signal "OK" and Sarge had the other guys bring the load out of the car in one trip. It took over an hour for the heat from the stove to thaw the ice on the inside of the windows. The mattress covers on the metal bunks against the walls stayed frozen solid just as long. No one was in a hurry to unpack their gear.

Sarge announced that this was a great time to complete our homework. He began to read from the Scout "Handbook for Boys", page 118, "Scout Spirit and Citizenship". He read about the Scout Code and how it shared principles with many historical documents from the Athenian Oath written three hundred years before the birth of Christ to the Declaration of Independence, Bill of Rights and the Constitution. He read the part about our country providing opportunities greater than any place on earth and how we did nothing to earn them and the debt we owe to Washington's soldiers who froze at Valley Forge and those who died in Europe and the Pacific. He told us we would repay that debt by preserving what they died for. We looked at him when he said it and we believed because he lived it and because it felt right. He read directly from the Handbook:

> "This country is today the unbelievable dream of millions of suffering people in other lands. Here are luxuries unheard of by them that you accept as a matter of course. Here are freedoms of which they

do not know the meaning. The American people speak as they think, worship as they choose, work where they wish and publish and read what they want. As a citizen of the United States of America it is yours to use rightly now and to transmit to those who come after you. Work for the satisfaction of accomplishment and self respect is the measure of the greatness of a purpose or nation. America is the land of opportunity-the opportunity to work and achieve a goal."

The games started. A wood match was placed tip up in the split on a piece of fire wood. The hatchet was passed around and we took turns chopping with it. The hatchet took the place of the striking pad. If you were good you could light the match by a glancing blow. If you were off you either missed it entirely or split it without lighting it. If you were really good you graduated to a long handled ax. Karl and Rocco used the ax. Leg wrestling commenced. I was usually the one who was goaded into being the first to lie on my back on the floor waiting for an opponent. I didn't lose unless I wanted to. Karl pushed Steinman forward. No athlete, he was 6 inches shorter than me which put him at a disadvantage to begin with. He got down next to me, side to side we faced each other, our left arms grasping the other guy's. On the count of three we raised our legs straight up like we were doing a hamstring stretch. The third time we did it we locked the legs up as they came down. If the stronger hooked up right he could push the other guys leg back toward his shoulder which resulted in the loser watching his ass go over his head as he was forced to execute a back flip. I put Steinman into the spectators the first hook up. This produced the usual grin of satisfaction from Karl. The second time around I let Steinman have the advantage by keeping my leg back and letting him push me the rest of the way. I made sure he won but I was not doing a back flip for anybody.

After we had a chance to warm up Sarge called for Karl, Rocco and me and told us to handle the water hole. We dressed and left the others packed around the stove making sure they did not lock the door from the inside. We stepped outside into a different world. The cabin was close to the lake and it took only a minute to slide down the last drop to the lake's edge. In front of us was the shining ice swept clean of snow by the blowing wind and lit by a million stars, invisible, and lost within the lights when we were in the city. The luminescent disc of a moon was pierced by a pine tree in this perfect valley. There we found the rope attached to a tree and a wood ladder, at the ready in case we misjudged the thickness of the ice. Rocco started the ax chopping through 8 inches of ice, handed it to me and finally Karl finished it. We worked fast because it was too damn cold. 3 buckets of water filled, we returned to a warm cabin. Sarge made sure we returned and only then, headed for the kitchen alcove, his domain, where he cracked open his flask of manhattans. Karl announced "lights out" and we retired to our semi-thawed bunks and sleeping bags.

Karl had selected his victim for the night. He waited until everyone was asleep then headed for Steinman with a cup of warm water. Steinman slept on the top bunk over the top of another kid. Karl slowly poured the water over Steinman's crotch until it leaked down on the kid in the bottom bunk. All hell broke loose and Karl shouted in mock terror, "Jesus Christ Steinman you pissed yourself again." Steinman never slept in a top bunk again. Years later he and Karl re-met at a class reunion. By that time Steinman was a nationally known microbiologist. Karl headed for him across the room, primarily because he wanted to know more about the beauty who was holding his arm. The diamond she wore was large and perfect. She was not amused when Karl steered the conversation to that night when Steinman earned the nick name "water boy". Mission accomplished, Karl walked away, smiling smugly and headed back to the bar where he had spotted a former cheerleader.

The camp is gone now. It was taken from the Boy Scouts by the government when they dreamed up the Tock's Dam Project to dam up the Delaware River. They never built it.

WALK LIKE A MAN

Frankie Valli and The Four Seasons

The southern boundary of our world was Shoretown. My Grandfather owned a cottage on a river about a mile from the ocean. When I was very young I slept in a bedroom on the water side. I went to sleep to the sound of an occasional car humming over the steel grating on the old bridge down at the end where fresh water met the salt of the bay. I grew up summers without shoes from June until August, treading across pine needles to get to the only food store out on the main road. I lived as much in and on the water as I did on the land. By age 10 I had boats with motors and my world was opened. There were no boat licenses, no age limits to operate one and I was free. Today people line up in boats to get through that opening after spending hours lined up in cars on the Parkway followed by lining up next to each other in marinas so they can line up next to each other and anchor. I was alone 90% of the time. If my Grandmother didn't need me to go to the store I was out the door and headed for the boat. I headed down river toward the ocean and turned to port toward the creek where the bridge lived.

This was my private place. It supplied everything a boy of ten could want. Blue claw crabs were scooped off the pilings that held it up. I caught many a snapper, blue fish and flounder and learned when the current was right to do it. I had my first close call with mortality there when I went over the side to free my anchor that had gotten caught on a sunken tree trunk. The branches caught a lot of fishing line as well as my anchor. Holding my breath in 10 feet of water I tangled up in the lines. If they had been modern monofilament I would have been sliced to ribbons pulling free. But they were braided cloth and I managed to pull free with a few minor abrasions. When you are ten, suppressing the breathing reflex because you are at the end of your air, the light on the surface of the water 6 feet over your head looks like a mile. It was the first of many true boating adventures that tested me. From that day forward I will not get on a boat without a knife.

The summer of 1962 I was fifteen. It was the last time I spent any real time in Shoretown. I was life guarding back in West Orange and only had one day off a week. Karl didn't have to work and had been pestering me to go to the shore. On my day off I coerced my Grandfather into driving us down for the day, staying overnight and driving us back the next day. Karl had a shit eating grin on his face all the way down. He told me to fire up the boat. By that time I had a fiberglass Glastron ski boat with a Mercury 75 horse motor. If you wanted speed you went with Mercury. If you wanted reliability you went with Evinrude. We went with Mercury. He directed me to the bridge. I tied up to the bulkhead and he headed up the road. He was gone about a half hour but it was worth the wait. He returned with a couple of six packs and two girls. I don't know how or where he got the beer, but he told me he knew the girls were vacationing here all summer and he had promised them a boat ride. To a fifteen year old guy a fast boat, beer and a tight, tanned, fifteen year old girl with long hair wearing a two piece and slathered in sun tan oil is sensory overload. Intoxicating. After riding around for a while we ended up on Treasure Island and Karl took his girl up the beach and into the trees. I was in the boat with mine and we made out for what seemed like hours. About the time it became clear it wasn't going any further Karl reappeared with his girl. He had taken the sure thing and needed me to get him there and separate her from her girlfriend. We drove them back to the bridge and they disappeared up onto the road. I don't remember their names and I never saw them again. The old bridge with the steel grate road was replaced long ago.

Before I hit my teens I had two nicknames. Karl dubbed me "Fatty". My body was the product of my grandmother's good German cooking and my mother's English upbringing of "eat everything in front of you, you don't know when you'll eat again." I was a good athlete and carrying extra weight was o.k. I didn't care if I was called "Fatty". The school gym teachers picked the captains who picked the teams for whatever it was we were going to play and the captains always picked me or Rocco right after Karl. Some of the kids weren't as lucky. We called one kid "Hands". You could place a baseball in his hands and he would drop it. Playing sports for him was not a remote possibility. He was lucky if he got one foot in front of the other. However, he played the best rock piano known to man. If you check out our yearbook you will find a picture of him dazzling the girls at the senior prom. When he was picked last in gym he just smiled. He knew he was a lousy athlete, we knew he was a lousy athlete, he laughed, we laughed and sometimes, as a joke on the gym teacher he got picked first. He went on to be keyboard player in at least 2 really popular Jersey Shore bands. Other differences weren't so obvious. We knew who was poor. We knew who was gay though we didn't talk about it. We knew who couldn't pass a math test. We knew who was painfully shy. The Home Coming Queen and King were thought to be the best looking and most popular. If you weren't the most popular you found your group and no one else seemed to care. Karl also dubbed me "Fungus" and I heard often, "there is a Fungus among us," Very cute. Karl thought it up because it rhymed with my name. No big deal. I was learning Karl had a streak that way.

Karl had a real shot at a college scholarship, not that he needed it. His father had money and their house was up the mountain on the other side of the woods from where I lived. By now our lives revolved around South Mountain Arena and ice hockey. When we weren't playing we were skating. Karl played center on the first line and we knew he was being scouted by Dartmouth. He also had 2 wing men who could make him look good, me and Rocco. I started working summers as a lifeguard at 15. The YMCA and years in the woods hardened me. The man kicked in. At 16 I was 6' and 175lbs with no fat left on me. Rocco was more compact, faster on skates then I was and a great stick handler. I had a greater reach and better anticipation. I also enjoyed the physical contact. I don't know why that happened but I do know when. I could have swum on the swim team my first year of high school but instead I chose hockey. The swim team won the state championship and hockey lost 9 games straight with me in the goal. Karl called the shot and moved me up to his line. Instead of people taking shots at me I was taking shots at them. Halfway during the first shift on the ice as a forward I got really pissed off. I was sick of losing. I put more effort into winning then I ever had in my life. I chased the puck into the corners and crashed guys into the boards and covered more ice than I ever had. Karl asked me between shifts, "What the hell got into you?" I told him I was sick of losing. He harnessed this. From then on my job was to hit and hit a lot. Rocco scooped up the puck if I didn't get to it and we fed it to Karl. Karl soon led the league in scoring as a junior.

Hockey practice was 6am three days a week and I could count on Reggie to be in front of my house in his 1953 Chevy convertible with Karl and Rocco. The hour was rough for us, but the figure skaters had it rougher. They had been on the ice since 4. The rink produced an Olympic champion, Carol Heise Jennings. Rocco usually led us in and cracked us up when he saw his sister Annie. "Hey, Annie, get off the ice we got work to do heah!" She flipped him the bird while maintaining a perfect Flying Camel. A radio in a car was a big deal. When Reggie made a metal bracket and mounted a reel to reel tape deck about the size of a suitcase under the dash it was a quantum leap forward. Frankie Valli and Connie Francis grew up 5 miles away from West Orange. Dionne Warwick's family with Matriarch Sissy Houston did too. I remember a singer friend of mine saying, "You think Dionne can sing? Wait until you hear this kid Whitney Houston." Reggie would tape songs off the radio by placing a microphone in front of the radio speaker and spending hours sitting on the edge of his chair ready to hit the "record" button when a song came on he wanted to record. We would blast The Four Seasons all the way to the rink. Soon after he got the reel to reel mounted the 8 track arrived. Reggie removed the suitcase, installed the

8 track and Karl could get his knees under the dash board again.

We had the most personable disc jockeys of all time. Scott Muni, Cousin Brucie and others like them were the face of our culture. The "Top 40" stations spoke to us anytime we were with our wheels or in our rooms. They selected what we heard. Vinyl records were expensive so we listened to the Jocks. I made it a point to listen after 9pm. Allison Steele, "The Night Bird", called to me from her studio in New York, sultry, sexy, soulful and mellow she was calling me, just me, me and Allison. She beckoned, "Come, fly with me", and I answered, "Yes Allison, I am ready. Take me anywhere." The Siren sang and I was drawn in. I had no idea what she looked like. This was an open invitation to leave boyhood behind. Most of us were ready.

That summer, between Junior and Senior year, became the most important of our lives. At some point our adolescent brains realized there was a world beyond high school. This was also when Father James began to hang out with us. He had taken a job working in the food stand at the club where I life guarded. We walked to and from the club together and had plenty of time to talk. He told me that the times he spent looking out the window at the other kid's playing weren't so bad. The cloistering was his apprenticeship to study for the priesthood and Mother had shown him there was so much to learn. He had been under tight rein for so long, had undergone so much indoctrination and was so sheltered that he had more reason to rebel than any of us did. But her plans for him had become a part of his personality. He couldn't wait to channel his life into one of sacrifice and service. She could afford to give him a little rope, confident she had done her job well. He had never played our sports, he was never allowed to be a scout, he never went to the YMCA, he never stuck his thumb out and hitch-hiked. She calculated that he would see how we lived and prefer the life chosen for him. She was right. From the day he began to hang out with us he was called "Father". Father James was an observer more than a participant. He amused Karl.

I realize now how good Karl was at reading people and putting them to his use. It was Karl who told me, "You got it, you just don't use it. You need someone like me to kick you in the ass." I floated, Karl focused. Rocco internalized, Karl identified and used.

Rocco knew he was different. He struggled badly with school. Today he would be classified, probably with ADHD, but we didn't know what that was in 1960. He was put into every shop and automotive class he could attend and at those he excelled. He could visualize, analyze and plan in his mind's eye and he could do amazing things. He wandered through childhood almost entirely within himself so consumed by the endless stream of thoughts in his head that it was if the outside world could not intrude. When something did get his attention all the energy that he had been internalizing during his down time from the external world was released at once. When he grabbed onto a project he shook it like a pit bull. Before he met us he got picked on a lot because he was quiet and distant. It was during one of Rocco's trips to reality that he was beating a tormentor senseless. Karl, who had never met him, pulled him off and led him away. Two minutes later it was as if nothing had happened. Karl introduced Rocco to me. We joined Scouts, Rocco joined Scouts. We played hockey, Rocco played hockey. We said, "We're going" and he followed. The external symptoms lessened as Rocco aged and that creative mind grew.

Cars were the key for transitioning to adulthood for adolescent males of the suburbs. My father drove a station wagon because of his work. My mother worked too, a rarity in the 1960's, but she worked with her father in his second generation store in Newark and it was accepted as normal. She had an Oldsmobile 88. Becoming eligible to get a learner's permit was one of the greatest days of my life. My friend Eugene already had his license and owned a Plymouth sedan with a combination stick shift and automatic. Yeah, in the 1960's the technology existed. I learned to drive in that car. When you have to work a clutch and gear shift you learn how to drive not just point a 3,000 lb. hunk of metal.

I can't recall if that car had power steering which was usually an option. It did have a really big but skinny steering wheel inside of which was a thin chrome bar that was the horn. The high beam switch was a button on the floor to the left of the clutch pedal. If you wanted more heat you pulled a lever that manually opened flaps on the air vents. The windshield wipers weren't electric. They were vacuum operated and a pain in the ass when you had the gas floored or were going up a hill because they would stop working until you took the load off the engine.

Bunky, took a 1949 Hudson and modified it. The interior was rolled and pleated white leather. The top of the car was cut off, lowered 8 inches and put back on. The suspension was chopped and the car lowered so that it cleared the pavement by 3 inches. The guy who applied the 13 coats of purple lacquer swore that was the last time he would do a job like that. Bunky went to work on the engine. Mufflers were replaced by straight exhaust pipes to relieve back pressure. He mounted "tripower", 3 carbs replacing the one four barrel that was stock. He gained horsepower but not braking and he put it under a tractor trailer on the Jersey Turnpike. That car was used for years, dropped off at the high school and left on the lawn before the senior prom as an example of what could happen. Bunky lived on in the blood stain they couldn't or wouldn't take off the white front seat. In driver education we were subjected to a movie called "Signal 13" which ran for 2 hours and showed every gory accident you could think of. The one that got us all was the poor dude who ran a truck into a wall while hauling a load of pipe. When the pipe came forward, through the cab, it crushed him against the wheel and then the pipe crushed him and the wheel against the dash. He compressed to the thickness of our math book.

Karl's father made sure he had the slickest '55 Chevy coupe ever seen. He went for the clean look. In those days there was chrome everywhere on a car. He removed every piece of chrome, except for the bumpers. The car was painted deep maroon and the finish was so deep it was like looking into molten metal. The hub caps were "moon discs", plain round chrome orbs completely covering all the wheel but the actual tire. From the side the effect was to see a maroon shape floating on 2 discs. From the front or back those chrome bumpers made it looked like it was floating on a chrome platform. The door handles were gone and the doors were hinged from the back making them "suicide doors". You entered by locating a button under the front wheel well which powered a solenoid in the trunk that popped the doors open. If the battery went dead you couldn't get into the car.

By now Father James and I were walking up the hill to Karl's where we got a ride to school every day with him and Rocco. I knew more about Father then they did because of my longer time spent with him and I felt sorry. Here was a guy monotracked and locked into the rest of his life on a direct path that took him to seminary and a life as a celibate. Our nostrils flared like bulls at the site of a girl showing some skin. I hadn't even thought about college. I was too busy experimenting with the possibilities of new experience. My parent's had never gone to college, never taught me to study, never wanted to see my homework and I cruised along getting "c"'s without opening a book.

Karl delighted in teasing Father and sometimes his taunts crossed the line as far as I was thinking. Father played violin in the school orchestra. His mother had made sure he had musical training and only classical would do. There would be no marching band, no dance band, no brass, no drums. The soulful beauty of the violin fit exactly. Deborah was also in the orchestra and she was known to any of the guys who knew anything as "Thunder Bunny". Her specialty was to break in first timers and she was always available. Not known to me, Karl had arranged to have Thunder Bunny introduce herself to Father. I arrived early for orchestra practice expecting to see Father there early also. There was Father being pressed against the drapes by Thunder Bunny who was whispering in his ear. He was frozen with a look I had never seen on him before. He was terrified and the pleading in his eyes was one of the most pathetic things I have ever seen. I walked up and touched her on the shoulder. She moved her head only so slightly and said to me, "James and I were just getting better acquainted." She knew me well. She had pitched me at the club the first year I life guarded. I told her I was going out with the girl guard, Dottie. Thunder Bunny respected that and left me alone. She got her kicks by breaking guys in and James was a challenge. She disengaged herself from him and turned and walked out. Father looked like he was standing on the edge of a cliff, terrified that he might jump. He remained rigid and breathing hard watching her walk away until I talked him down. She didn't approach him in school again as far I know.

A month later we were playing the last hockey game of our high school careers. We had brought Father further into our lives by having coach make him equipment manager. His mother thought that was splendid. One of the perks of being a senior was that you could drive your car instead of taking the team bus. Of course, we rode with Karl. There were times when Karl didn't invite us to ride in that maroon Chevy. Karl had all the action he wanted and a lot of it he got behind the arena, in the Chevy, with girls he met during the public skating sessions. He had his usual parking spot, all the way in the back under the pine trees.

We won our last game and lingered on the ice after the visiting team left. It was ended and I wanted to savor all the things I would miss, the excitement of physical play, the crowded stands, the feeling you get when it is ended and you are tired and satisfied. We headed for the locker room. I unlaced the skates and I stripped out of the Jersey and pads. Coming out of the shower I saw Father already headed out the door that emptied from the locker room directly to the outside of the building.

"Where is he going?", I asked Karl.

"I sent him out to my car. Told him to bring it around to the front. I arranged a little surprise for him."

Karl didn't smile when he said that and I didn't like it. I grabbed my clothes and dressed as quick as I could and headed toward the car, but I was already too late. Father had arrived at the car and Thunder Bunny stepped from behind a pine tree to meet him. He was already by the front fender trying to find the switch that opened the door when she surprised him. She turned him around, put his back against the fender and pressed against him.

"I would just love to make you happy darlin'. Let me work my magic".

Father was paralyzed. She kept her hips against him pinning him to the fender. Her eyes never left his. He was petrified, she knew it and she loved it.

"Come on damn it, get the door open," she said as she wrapped herself around him and felt for the switch in the wheel well.

He wanted to move. He couldn't move. He wanted to be anywhere but here.

At that moment the headlights from the team bus caught the back of the car as the bus made a wide turn through the back parking lot and headed for the front of the arena. Thunder Bunny and James didn't know that only the driver was in the bus and that he had seen nothing but the back of the '55. I arrived at the same time and caught Thunder Bunny before she could get off of Father. She smiled at me and slowly moved back letting her hand run down the front of his shirt. James didn't moved off the fender even though she was off him. She kept looking me right in the eyes until she was turned and slinking into the trees. Father was still as rigid as a statue when I took him by the arm and we started walking. The team didn't have an equipment manager to pack up. And they didn't have me. This was not how I wanted to remember my last game. He said nothing and neither did I. When we got to his house he said, "Thanks", that was it, "Thanks." Karl and I never had the same relationship. Years smashed.

Karl walked to the '55. Thunder Bunny was already in the back seat. He couldn't wait to have her tell him about it, every detail. She made up a lot of shit and told it to him hoping it would turn him on.

I left Father James and headed home. My father's friend was supposed to pick me up and we would drive to the hunting camp in Pennsylvania. I was the only guy under 40 invited to hunt with this group of veterans. I was allowed because they needed someone to walk the deer into their guns. The camp was a farm owned by the former national rifle champion of Germany. Hitler came in and he got out. His machine shop made the bomb sights for the American bombers that blew Germany all to hell. His son couldn't attend public school. Because of his German name and accent he got the crap kicked out of him.

I discovered the pain in my knee while walking Father James home. Don't know at what point in the game it went south, but it hurt like hell now. I was in lousy shape mentally and physically.

"Mom, I am gonna call Otto and tell him I am not going." It was 9:30pm, the drive was three hours and breakfast was at 4am before hitting the mountain. I was fried.

My father returned the next day instead of Sunday. "You won't believe this. I thought about how to tell you but here it comes straight: Otto hit the side of the bridge in Honesdale and is dead."

There but for the grace of God and circumstance went I.

THAT'S WHY GOD MADE THE RADIO
The Beach Boys
SHE'S MY LITTLE DEUCE COUPE

My ride was a 1953 Chevy convertible that needed work, the same car Reggie picked us up in until I bought it. He was headed for the Air Force and dumped it. I paid him $225. It was a butt ugly faded turquoise with dark blue seats. The convertible top was white and in good shape. The metal frame for it was a bear. It bent when I picked up one side and it was tough to put back up if I was alone. I don't know if any car of that year had a power top, but this one didn't. The coolest one I ever saw was a powered folding hard top convertible where the hard roof separated into sections that folded into the trunk. Way cool. Reggie took the stick shift off the column and installed a Hearst floor shifter. Under the hood was an anemic straight six cylinder that left enough room in the engine compartment to seat two people. I did the best I could with it. We gave it a new carburetor, straight tail pipes and "Cherry Bomb" mufflers instead of the stock silencers. I made it through inspection that way. Everyone knew the story of Bunky trying pass inspection with his straight pipes. He had wrapped coat hangers with steel wool and slid them up the tail pipes figuring the sound would be deadened enough to pass without mufflers. He didn't figure the inspection guys had mirrors on a stick that checked the underside of the car. They had seen it all a hundred times and when they saw no mufflers and a quite running car they knew what to do. The inspector floored it in neutral and blew the steel wool out of the pipes like a spear out of a spear gun. Bunky failed. When he put it under that truck it had that "failed" inspection sticker on the windshield. My father brought home one of the guys from the shop who taped off the trim on my car and shot it with dark blue paint. I buffed it out with a grinder and a buffing pad. The finishing touch was a pair of dice I had won at a boardwalk stand hanging from the mirror. My father put it in the shop, paid for brakes and new tires and gave it back to me.

I was ready for my right of passage. I called up Dottie, the girl guard from the club. Her father answered the phone.

"Yes, young man, and what is your name?" "Just a moment. I'll see if she is available. Dorothy, there is a young man on the phone who wishes to speak with you."

Dottie picked up. "Hang up Daddy. I have it." She made sure he hung up the downstairs phone before we talked.

"I haven't heard from you for a while. I thought you forgot about me." "I couldn't forget about you, but different schools is tough and I had a lot going on."

I told her I hadn't dated anyone and how much I enjoyed being around her last summer. All that was the truth. We agreed on Saturday night and it would be the Livingston Drive-In. She told her father and mother we were going to the movies. "How nice dear." Yes, it certainly was.

For us the drive-in movie was a right of passage. You got a car, you got a girl, you went to the drive-in. Saturday night we sat in the line of cars paying the admission fee. Each car paid at the booth and popped the trunk to prove there were no freebies hitching a ride in. The side of the stories high screen could be seen from Route 10. In selecting an outdoor movie there was one main criteria: Did the patrolling ranger leave the kids steaming up car windows alone?

Considering Bunky was the ranger, may he rest in peace, I had it covered. Dottie looked great, smelled great and the conversation was easy. After driving through the booth I selected a place on the gravel infield. You never parked near the projection booth or the food stand, too much foot traffic. You never parked in the back row. Only the really dumb parked there thinking the further away the better. That is the first place the ranger went to bang on windows. You parked in the middle, with an empty space on either side, hoping that the next car passed by and left it empty. Couples with kids didn't live by this code and there was always a chance you had someone next to you. After successfully docking within reach of the speaker on a post, you removed it and attached it to the inside of the driver's side window. In the summer the problem was always the heat with the windows rolled up. In the winter it was the need to run the engine to get some heat. Alcohol was strictly forbidden. Dottie asked if I had any and I produced the pint of black berry brandy taken from my father's hunting gear locker. I was set up: Front wheels of the car elevated on the berm with a great angle to the screen, speaker inside and window rolled up, empty space on both sides of the car, nice fall night, blackberry brandy and a girl.

It was the first time I did more than make out. She was warm, willing and it was easy. I was with Dottie for the rest of the senior year and we really liked each other. She graduated the week before my school did. She was actually the one to say goodbye, headed for Vermont for the summer and then college there. Great girl. I never saw her again.

NIGHT MOVES

Bob Seeger

Karl, Roccco, Father James and I were only together one more time. Graduation passed, the parties were over and we decided to go to the shore and the boardwalk together. We all knew it was the probably the last time for all of us, but no one said anything. First time for Father. Boardwalks were originally invented for hotels as a way to have people coming off the beach drop the sand off their feet before entering. They are simply cross boards with space in between for the sand to drop off. The Point Pleasant boardwalk was built on telephone poll posts 4 feet above the sand and ran for one mile from the inlet south. My parents started taking me there when I was just big enough for the kiddie rides. The food concessions and amusement games were in the middle of the mile. A perpetual railing ran the length of the ocean side with steps that led down to the sand beach that stretched a hundred yards to the surf. Every time I think of it I smell the pizza and sausage and onions mixed with the smell of the salt off the ocean. I hear the sounds of people on the rides, bells and gongs going off as people played the boardwalk games. Bruce Springsteen captured it all when Danny lit it up with his boardwalk organ.

Turf was important. The day I got my varsity jacket was huge. Our colors were maroon and white. The wool maroon jacket had white leather sleeves with my name and small crossed hockey sticks on the front. The back was covered by the school initials and larger crossed sticks. We wore them everywhere and walked with pride. Football, wrestling and hockey were the big three, physical contact sports that were a notch up in the pecking order. Basketball had not yet evolved into a physical game and we had no idea why anyone would wear a golf varsity jacket.

The boardwalk was home turf for the shore kids. The railing dead center across from the frozen custard stand was reserved for them. The summer cops were hired to keep the boardwalk rules enforced ignored these guys and they sat on the railings, a clear violation of the law. We were lost in the action and oblivious when we walked past them. I was in the middle, inside of Father, when he was rammed into me by the local blue and white varsity jacket who was "pushed" by his buddy still sitting on the railing. I grabbed Father by the elbow and we kept walking. "Just keep walking", said Karl. The insults from the five locals faded as we got lost in the moving crowd.

We were pissed. Karl came up with the plan. Father was not equipped to handle what we would do next. We cut in behind the haunted house which stuck out into the boardwalk. We stripped off our jackets and Karl told Father to hold them. He could just see the railing where our antagonists were when he looked around the corner. We hopped the railing and crossed under the boardwalk to the ocean side. We stayed under the boards, hunched over and headed for the railing where the blue and whites were. Five of them, three of us. Karl in the middle flanked by me and Rocco. We wasted no time. They were leaning forward and it was easy to grab the back of their belts and pull them backwards off the railing. I took two, Rocco took two and Karl grabbed the one in the middle. Karl got the most leverage and I think his guy was out or maybe just dazed when the back of his head hit the sand. The other four never stood a chance. We were on top beating the shit out of them. One of mine never got off his back and covered up. That is the one Karl beat on. I made short work of the other. I had him by the front of his shirt with my left hand. That is the only way I knew how to fight, hockey style, grab with one hand, use it to keep him off balance and pummel with the right. I missed with a right hand but my elbow caught him on the bridge of the nose and I heard it crack. I'd seen a lot of blood, but I never saw a nose bleed like that. I dropped him and looked over to see Rocco standing over the other two. Karl was wailing on this guy, freaking beating his face into a pulp. I hauled him off but he wouldn't stop. Rocco jumped in and we grabbed Karl who got in a final kick as we ran back up the sand under the boards like the hunchbacks of Notre Dame. Father met us. "Oh, my God!" was all he could say.

We never stopped to look back until we had crossed the boardwalk and found the '55. We talked to Karl to keep him under control as he drove out of town. He wouldn't let it go and his expression scared me. It took only a minute to cross the two lane high arched bridge up by the inlet and drive directly away from the ocean. Then we stopped in a bar parking lot, the energy still pumping, the lights brighter, the sounds louder and we assessed the damage. Rocco had a cut lip. I was unmarked. Karl's right hand was a mess. We put the jackets on and cruised out of town euphoric, except for Father, who was a mental disaster. That was the last time the four of us were together.

Two days later Rocco and I put camping gear in the convertible, bought a map of the U.S. and started driving to California. I had saved up enough money from guarding and working part time for my grandfather to make it happen. Gas was 32 cents a gallon and we figured we would sleep in a tent or in the car. In September I was headed for a college in the Midwest that actually accepted a mediocre student athlete with a grade point average of 2.1. Rocco was headed for a couple of years of pouring concrete with a kid who graduated a year before us. This was OUR summer and the last chance to let it rip before we got serious.

I am not Jack Kerouac and we had no motivation when we drove west other than to see the country. When we came back we had been coast to coast at age 18 but had no idea where we were going.

BE TRUE TO YOUR SCHOOL

The Beach Boys

In the Fall of 1964 Karl got himself situated at college in New Hampshire. It didn't take him long to let it be known that he was a scholarship hockey player and someone to be reckoned with even if he was a freshman. His parents staked him to an apartment just off campus and that made him an instant BMOC, "big man on campus". His pad became the social center for the hockey team. Within weeks he had one of the smartest ladies in the school doing his course work and writing his papers. That left him plenty of time to memorize the stuff he knew his professors wanted regurgitated. He recruited another lady to keep the place clean and provide him with fringe benefits. The off campus parties at his place had him cultivating groupies like a rock star. He managed to keep them all separated and feeling like they were really important to him.

In 1965 there were no cell phones, no computers for the masses and no social network. If you wanted to contact someone over distance you called a land line phone. I would have had to find out the area code for his town and call information there to see if the operator could look up a phone number in his name. I didn't want to keep in touch with him anyway.

Father James enrolled in Seton Hall University's summer session right after high school graduation. It would take him 3 years to obtain his degree in divinity and then enter seminary if he took no breaks. That was the plan. He attended college only a couple of miles from home. When he was not in school or church he was at the mission on Springfield Avenue, Newark. That was his life. He studied and attended class non-stop. He made sure he devoted an hour a day to cooking and handing out food at the mission. Sundays, all day, were spent in church. He visited as many Catholic churches in the Oranges as he could. He studied the priests and observed. 18 years old and he was already a servant of Christ. His mother was ecstatic. I saw Father James when I came home for Christmas break and during the summer. Our street was still home to us and I stayed with my parents when I wasn't in the Midwest. After taking off that one summer to drive across the country, I continued to life guard at the country club on top of the mountain and descended into Newark to work at my Grandfather's store June to September. Father James mission was one block further east of Grandpa's store on Springfield Avenue and our paths crossed often. His conversation never varied from religion and service and after a while it sounded like a broken record to me.

I had grown up in St. Cloud Presbyterian Church which I attended with my parents most Sundays. That is where our scout troop met. We went through a series of ministers, I as a child, not knowing anything of politics or the realities of finances that even a church has to deal with. For me the church community was a calming sense of belonging and familiarity. The neighborhood, the school, the church, Scouts, all this was suburban utopia. We were insulated in our own microcosm, in a cocoon of perfect post World War II middle class life. A boy in his formative years gets lucky if he is blessed with a special person. I was surrounded by strong males beginning with my father. When I was 15 Dr. Gerry Mills took St. Cloud as his first church and he and his wife Judy changed lives. Gerry is a converted Jew who had fully accepted Jesus as Savior. It was a shock to the elders who hired him when he put curtains with Hebrew character letters in his office.

It was all about inclusion, joy and a positive energy that brought in kids from all over the neighborhood. I looked at Father James' religious experience as rigid and joyless and suffocated by dogma. I absorbed the energy and spirituality and pure joy the Mills radiated.

When we were kids everyone in our neighborhood knew Grounhawg. That's what his business card said, one word, "Grounhawg". I guess it wasn't really a business card because it didn't have even a phone number. It was more like a greeting card. He was a tall, skinny, black guy who drove up into West Orange from Newark six days a week in a tattered station wagon loaded with hand tools, a ladder strapped to the roof and a wheelbarrow that barely fit inside. I would guess he was about 30 when we were in high school. It was tough to tell. His smile never left his face and the neighbors kept him busy. He would take on any manual task and do it for a fair price. His specialty was masonry and he was always patient when kids came around to see what he was doing. Rocco never missed an opportunity to learn from him and Grounhawg patiently answered Rocco's stream of questions about building things. There was no college in sight for Rocco. (A) He had no interest in college. (B) He could never have passed the courses. (C) Why go to college when you have golden hands, an aptitude for mechanical things, boundless energy and the ability to design in your mind? Rocco was going to work for a guy, but Grounhawg had started to use Rocco for jobs that went faster with four hands in our junior year. Grounhawg quickly found out that he had a huge advantage if Rocco worked with him. Grounhawg was well known and respected in our neighborhood, but get him out of there and he was met with doubt and sometimes prejudice. Grounhawg had his pride and Rocco knew it and looked up to him for his knowledge of construction and how to work out problems. Under Grounhawg's nurturing Rocco's talents began to emerge. Grounhawg quickly learned Rocco could fix anything mechanical, invent ways to do jobs quicker and figure complex situations in his head. Rocco became the front man at the age of 19. Customers meeting the duo for the first time assumed Rocco was the boss and Grounhawg was the laborer. Grounhawg smiled, making more money than he ever had in his life. By 1967 their business card read:

G and R Construction
Residential & Commercial
No job too big, No job too small.
Call Rocco: 732-2775

Grounhawg used the station wagon every morning to get to the two car garage and fenced in yard that held their ever growing inventory of equipment. They traveled in Rocco's brand new pick up truck with the gold lettered signs on the doors. Rocco was a workhorse who wanted to spend his time in the field playing with his toys. His toys got bigger and so did the jobs. In a few years Grounhawg was running the crews and Rocco was running the heavy equipment. That led to an office staffed by an inside person doing the estimating and scheduling. In 1973 the first cell phone was invented. They were designed for a car because there was no way an individual could carry around 25 pounds of equipment. The base was hard wired into the trunk with a hole drilled for an external antenna. The base unit was too big to go anywhere else. The wires were run through the car to the front seat where the actual phone was. The part you talked into looked like a home phone. Rocco may have had the first truly remote cellphone in history. He took a metal tool box, mounted a 12 volt motorcycle battery next to the equipment and ran a magnet mount antenna on a long cord out the window of whatever car or truck he was taking at the time. Genius, always one step ahead.

As for me, the vibe at the small liberal arts college 30 miles from the Mississippi river was totally different than Jersey. I took a deep breath and slowed down. It wasn't just the pace of life, but attitude as well. Here was a sense of personal openness. People didn't seem as guarded. They weren't always rushing somewhere else. Part of it was the small college town atmosphere in the middle of farm country where they thought they knew you whether they did or not. Roads were empty and straight. Chicago was a weekend not a day trip. Iowa was across the Mississippi and there wasn't much more in Davenport then there was where I was at. I brought more experiences and faster pace than most of the other 18 year olds and that served me well.

When Rocco and I returned from California in the '53 Chevy she was pretty used up. I would have driven myself to college but freshman weren't allowed to have cars. I would not have regarded this as a challenge in New Jersey and would have found a place to keep one. But out there everyone knew everyone and they would have caught me. Where was I going anyway? My parents dropped me off at the dorm and I moved in with two other guys assigned alphabetically. The Gods were smiling. Luckily, one was from Connecticut, had the east coast edge and played guitar like a rock star. Thus commenced a frantic year of finding out that I could not possibly get involved in all the things people wanted to get me involved in and still pass my courses. By Christmas I had been working out with the swim team six days a week, was singing lead with an acoustical folk group, and was immersed in the music cultural transforming folk into rock. I had stumbled upon a guy from Syracuse who had an MG with low cut doors and we hung out at race tracks. Oh yeah, and I got a .67 in a 4 point grading system. Yes, a .67 in a 4 point system is possible. Whoops, time to re-calibrate.

My roommate figured out the cheapest and fastest way to get back to the east coast for the winter break. He had rounded up a guy from New York and a girl from Connecticut and bought a car from a farmer for $150. He had great taste in traveling companions but not so much in cars. I don't remember what kind of car it was but I do know that case of oil cans in the trunk impressed me. The four of us loaded up and launched out of town trailing a plume of blue smoke. This was not going to end well.

It is damn cold in Illinois in December. The heater worked sort of and, because the oil was burning off the heads of the engine, we had to ride with a back window down or risk asphyxiation. The girl never wanted for warmth because she was in the middle with a guy on either side of her snuggling up while one guy drove through the night. She was a sweet heart and by the end of the trip was one of the guys. 15 hours later we pulled up at my house. I took them to the gas station and we bought another case of oil. My parents were enveloped in the moving blue cloud as they waved goodbye to the three of them leaving to finish up the last couple hours of the trip.

They picked me up for the return as scheduled. It was obvious nothing had been done to the car other than there was now a case of "motor honey" next to the case of oil. Guaranteed to stop oil burning. Sure. Somewhere west of Chicago, in the middle of nowhere, on a totally straight black line, surrounded by absolutely nothing, in December, with a 30 mile an hour headwind blowing across nothing but dirt and the temperature hovering around zero there was a loud bang followed by a small fire that went out of its own accord about the time I steered this turkey to the shoulder. Great, we were going to freeze to death. I am sure the semi driver never expected to see a girl with long hair not wearing a hat or coat standing next to a smoking car. He stopped, we emerged, he laughed, we laughed, removed the license plates from the car, put the girl and two guys in his sleeper bunk behind the front seats and he actually diverted off the highway to drop us in front of the student union. I passed the girl on campus almost every day for the next three years and we cracked up every time we saw each other. The guy from New York was in culture shock, transferred after one year and my roommate flunked out.

I found the balance of passing courses while immersing myself in stuff I had never done before. By the Spring semester I had completed the swimming season, solid, but not one of the stars. Before my roommate flunked out he talked me into skydiving. We practiced landing by jumping off a 55 gallon oil drum. Then they took us up in a four seat Cessna wing-over with a pipe welded under the wing strut on the bottom of the door. I stepped out onto the pipe holding onto the wing strut and let go. This was a static line jump. The rip cord was attached to the plane and the chute would open when I reached the end of it. I was supposed to look up and arch my back. Not. I tucked my head and completed a forward roll as the chute came out. I have no idea how I did not get tangled up, but I didn't and landed it ok on the airport grounds in soft dirt. My roommate was not as lucky. He deployed perfectly and steered for the airport. The airport was bordered by a gravel road. He had the misfortune to come in over the road, barb wire fence a foot beneath his boots and overhead wires between him and the chute. He hung up, made one swing like a pendulum and landed backward on his heels in the road. 2 broken ankles don't help you be successful in college.

I look back in wonderment that the best fraternity on campus decided I should join. They were proud of their grade point average. I had work to do. I was mentored by men much wiser than I. We won everything. We had won the singing competition so many times in a row that we tried to throw it by doing a slap stick version of "Row, Row, Row Your Boat". We won. The quarterback on the College's football team was a Brother and got drafted into the NFL. We won the intramural Olympics and we won the grade point competition. I ended up on team everything and they carried me academically.

I left for Jersey at the beginning of June having found my college footing but knowing I needed the smell of salt water, my car and more adventures out of the Midwest. Before we left for summer break we had a going away party down by the Mississippi at an abandoned railroad bridge in the middle of nowhere. The locals knew the best places to party. A hundred college students were on the bridge, over the bridge, making out in cars and basically doing our best to consume all the liquor dumped into an old bathtub. You brought a bottle of something, you poured it into the tub with everything else that was dumped in and you were off. We had to party off campus. In those days the girls dorms had a curfew of 9pm on weeknights and 11pm on weekends. They had only one phone booth on the first floor and a matron that answered it, checked the girls in and out and basically kept them from having any fun. The party had been going on since 1 in the afternoon when, just as the sun was going down, we heard a siren. Coming down the dirt road was a black and white with a gumball machine on the roof rotating red. The car came to a halt and out stepped Barney Fife. We looked at him in total disbelief. He must have been sent by Andy, straight out of Mayberry and I am not sure his gun was loaded.

"For the love of Pete, what is this?", he bellowed in our general direction not to anyone in particular. One of the senior cheerleaders came to the rescue. "Why hello officer, can we help you with something?"

He focused on 5'9 inches of Midwestern WOMAN, wearing cut off denim shorts and a tee shirt, sort of. A couple of her buddies picked up on what was going on in a hurry and the party never slowed as he found himself surrounded by college coeds loosening his tie, taking his hat and tussling his hair and ready to show him a good time. He must have had one hell of a time, because I remember seeing him tied to the bridge railing wearing nothing but his jockeys when someone yelled we had to leave now to get the girls home by curfew. I hope they left his gun.

GRAZING IN THE GRASS

Hugh Masakala/Friends of Distinction

SWEET CAROLINE

Neil Diamond

The men friends, business associates and hunting companions of my father were a constant positive presence. So many of them wore the ring of a Freemason that I finally connected the dots and asked my father about Freemasonry. That was all I had to do. I was paid a visit by the lawyer who lived up the street and Gene, who had worked for my grandfather since WWII. They handed me a thin book on the history of Freemasonry, told me to read it and they would see me again.

The date that Freemasonry was founded is often debated. What is certain is that the oppressed will seek to change the old order. 1300-1400 AD was not a time to question the authority of the Church or the monarchies that were competing against each other for world domination. Enlightened men, humanists today, those interested in the good of the common man and the arts and sciences, could not openly speak out. To do so would be a challenge to Papal authority and royal families. It is logical to think that they met together as any group of men with common interests would. They could not have done this openly. The Grande Lodge of Scotland possesses the minutes of a lodge meeting from 1599. "Mother Lodge of Scotland" claims the ability to trace it's origins to the 12th Century.

Those who could move freely in the world were "operative" stone masons. Their trade was vital to church and state because they could build the great cathedrals and palaces of the two warring powers seeking control of man's hearts, bodies and minds. These guilds provided the template for "Speculative Freemasonry". The date of the actual origination of speculative freemasonry, a brotherhood of like minded humanists who joined these lodges, can not be pinpointed. The three elements visible to anyone who cares to look are the square, compass and the letter "G". The square and compass are the two essential working tools of a Master Mason and the letter "G" is for God. God is thought of as the grand architect of all that is. In Freemasonry God is not defined beyond that and each Mason is left to believe what he wishes about a supreme being. For that reason there are Masonic lodges in almost every civilized country and of any and all religions. Although the way in which lodges conduct business may vary and the ritual may be somewhat different, a man who wears a masonic ring recognizes a brother who deserves respect and friendship for similar humanistic beliefs.

An individual's obligation to his own moral compass, responsibility to his family and his community, and quest for continuing enlightenment transcends governments and churches. There are many documented stories of how men in opposing armies respected this bond, and aided a brother in distress. Go to Gettysburg Battlefield, seek and you shall find.

The "Craft" stands for the dignity of the individual, freedom from tyranny, the rights of all to worship as he sees fit, the importance of education and the desire for continual learning to bring "light" to lives. It is no wonder that Mozart, Beethoven, Voltaire, Alexander Pope, Sir Walter Scott, Sir Francis Bacon and likely Sir Isaac Newton were early Masons.

Then I read further and found that Daniel Carter Beard, who founded the Boy Scouts of America, was a Freemason. I had been raised by men who not only shared the values but who taught them. When I was made a Master Mason Rocco was on the sidelines, watching, when my grandfather took my hand and "raised" me. I joined the ranks of many who had come before. Some have made their mark on the world as public figures. Most go about their lives trying to be a positive influence. All are human. The Craft teaches responsibility to oneself, one's family and one's community. Not all succeed and some join for the wrong reasons thinking that power or prestige or political connections are advanced by doing so. But, if there is a worldwide organization with more noble humanistic goals I do not know of it.

A PARTIAL LIST WELL KNOWN FREEMASONS

U.S. Presidents: George Washington, James Monroe, Andrew Jackson, Theodore Roosevelt, William Taft, Warren Harding, James Polk, James Buchanon, Andrew Johnson, James Garfield, William McKinley, Franklin Roosevelt, Harry Truman, Lyndon Johnson (took the first of 3 degrees, never became a Master Mason), Gerald Ford

Military and Political Leaders: Winston Churchill, Tony Blair, King Hussein of Jordan, Yasser Arafat, Francois Metterand, Helmut Kohl, Reverend Jesse Jackson, Robert Dole, Jack Kemp, Strom Thurmond, Prince Phillip, Zbigniew Brzezinski, Andrew Carnegie, Henry Kissinger, Simon Bolivar, Benito Juarez, Jose de San Martin, Jose Marti, Pandit Nehru, George McGovern, Barry Goldwater, Thomas Dewey,

Hubert Humphry, William Jennings Bryant, John Paul Jones, General Omar Bradley, General Douglas Macarthur, General John Pershing, General Matthew Ridgeway, General Winfield Scott, Captain Eddie Rickenbacker, Jimmy Doolittle, Audie Murphy

Artists and Entertainers: William Shakespeare, Leonardo Da Vinci, W. A. Mozart, Leopold Mozart, Ludwig Van Beethoven, Franz List, Josef Hayden, Irving Berlin, Richard Wagner, Count Basie, Louis Armstrong, Nat King Cole, John Phillip Sousa, Gilbert and Sullivan, John Wayne, Red Skelton, Clark Gable, W.C. Fields, Oliver Hardy, Tom Mix, Audie Murphy, Will Rodgers, Burl Ives, Roy Rogers, Danny Thomas, Gene Autry, Ernest Borgnine, Wallace Beery, Eddy Cantor, Roy Clarke, George M. Cohan, Walt Disney, Duke Ellington, Douglas Fairbanks, Arthur Godfrey, Bob Hope, Harry Houdini, Will Rogers, Peter Sellers, Cecille B. DeMille, Brad Paisley, Little Jimmy Dickens, Roy Clark, legendary golfer Arnold Palmer

Industry and Banking: Henry Ford, Samuel Gompers, Walter Chrysler, Ransom Olds (Oldsmobile) Giovanni Agnelli (Fiat), John Wanamaker, S.S. Kresge, J.C. Penny, John Jacob Astor, Pehr Gyllenhammar (Volvo), Samuel Colt, Rockefeller family, Rothschild family, Charles Hilton, Dave Thomas (Wendys), Alan Greenspan

Adventurers: Lewis and Clarke, Charles Lindbergh, Kit Carson, Roald Amundson, Admiral Richard Byrd, Commodore Robert Perry, Buffalo Bill Cody, Davy Crocket, Robert Peary

Writers: Mark Twain, Sir Walter Scott, Rudyard Kipling, Robert Burns, Alexander Pushkin, Sir Arthur Conan Doyle, Jonathon Swift, Oscar Wilde, Jules Vern, H.G. Wells, Francis Scott Key, Alexander Pope

Science: Carl Sagan, Albert Einstein, Albert Michelson (measured speed of light), Alexandre Eiffel

Philosophers: Johann Wolfgang von Goethe, Gotthold E. Lessing, Voltaire

10 American Astronauts who had 'the right stuff': Buzz Aldren, Leroy Cooper, Donn Eisele, Virgil Grissom, Edgar Mitchell, Walter Shirra Jr., Thomas Stafford, Paul Weitz, James Irvin, John Glenn

This is a very partial list.

The Masonic Temple dominated Main Street, Orange. It was the highest structure on Main built of dark red stone with turrets at the top. My grandfather marched in the dedication parade in the 1800's. The Oranges and surrounding area played a major role in the founding of The United States. The opposing Continental and British armies crisscrossed New Jersey during the War for Independence. Washington had a tough day in New York City when he was out generalled, out flanked and barely escaped with what was left of his army, across the Hudson River. Orange has the "Military Commons" running down the center of Main Street where the retreating army camped. The well soldiers of both sides drank from is a depression in a paved parking lot and refuses to stay buried. The statue of the Dispatch Rider was erected on the corner of Main and Day at the church yard where British soldiers camped. My cousin was married in the church in neighboring Springfield where a cannon ball is still lodged in the wall. West Orange has "Tory Corner" and Eagle Rock where the Continentals had a clear view into New York from the top of our mountain.

Rocco and I poured over documents about the Revolution and the Lodge. When we heard the Vice President of the United States take his oath of office we were astounded to hear a phrase in the Oath taken almost verbatim from the Masonic ritual. We were surrounded by Masonic influence.

It was fitting that the Temple be the dominant building on Main, constructed only 100 years after the Revolution. Much has been said about Freemasonry's involvement in the founding of the United States. There are those who would seek to exaggerate the role organized Freemasonry played in the founding of this country and there are those who would play it down. When I was "raised" into that Lodge it became clear to me. The Masonic ideals and the way in which Masons conduct business was the foundation of a new, democratic government in the U.S., not because the Craft organized in some sort of grand conspiracy, but because of the ideals of the men who were Masons acting as individuals. There were many Masons who were on the British side. Modern Masonry can be traced to Scotland.

The Lodges recognized the worth and the rights of individuals. There all ranks were leveled. Lodges were common in the Continental Army and when they organized, military rank had nothing to do with who was elected to fill the officer's chairs. Military officers sat with privates. This was democracy.

Lodges were governed by a Constitution: They were constituted under warrant from a Grand Lodge and expected to conform to the rules of conduct, individualistic, but united.

Lodges, at the core, demand responsibility from the individual to basic values and his obligations to his country and to all mankind.

I have little doubt that Masonry had been a model for how a democratic government could function. Washington and all Freemasons involved in the Revolution shared the core values and the men in subsequent Lodges passed it on to me and those like me.

These are a few examples of the documented actions by Freemasons during the War For Independence: General Joseph Warren, Grand Master of Massachusetts was killed at Bunker Hill. His body was identified by his Lodge brother, Paul Revere.

It can be documented that 8 of the 56 signers of the Declaration of Independence were Masons. Another 6 were probably Masons but can not be proven.

George Washington was Master of his Lodge. Many of his Generals were Masons. He encouraged military lodges within the army. Van Steuben, the German General who drilled the raw Americans into a fighting force, was a German Freemason who came to help the American cause.

Benjamin Franklin was dispatched to France by the Continental Congress to bring France into the War on the American side. I found it astounding that Franklin became the Master of a French Freemason's Lodge. We won our War for Independence when Franklin convinced the French to be our allies. The French fleet and Continental Army cornered the British Army at Yorktown, Virginia in 1781. The British surrendered and we became independent.

The architect who designed Washington D.C. was a Freemason. When

George Washington placed the corner stone of the U.S. Capital in 1793 he was in full Masonic regalia. President Harry S. Truman, former Grand Master of Missouri, oversaw the reconstruction of the Capital and was delighted to find the cornerstone and many Masonic artifacts.

The Federal Government began The Washington Monument. When the Government stopped construction the Freemasons paid for and assured it's completion. The line where the Masons took over and finished the job the Government started is clearly visible. The stones that rise above the base, completing the Monument, came from a different quarry and are a slightly different color.

Freemasons don't forget to whom everyone in the U.S. owes their freedom and the price our ancestors paid to achieve it. If you are headed south on Route 95 and cross the Potomac River into Virginia look to your right on top of the hill and see The George Washington Masonic Memorial.

We felt a deep respect for the sacrifices made by our Brothers for us. We recognized that our principles were the same and that our generation had an obligation to preserve them. This was not only for the memory of those who gave these priceless gifts to us, but for all who came here seeking what our ancestors had paid a dear price for. We understood why our fathers and grandfathers, men of character, had been willing to fight and die. We thought all who lived here understood, appreciated and shared our values. We were wrong.

It was 1967 and our patriotism, our naive youthful view of the world and all we thought our country was, took a major hit. Our comfortable bubble was about to explode and we had been living next to it the whole time.

THE STAR SPANGLED BANNER

Francis Scott Key

AMERICA THE BEAUTIFUL

Composed in Grace Episcopal Church, Newark, NJ
by Samuel A. Ward, words by Katharine Lee Bates

Newark was founded in 1666 by the Puritans who named it "New Ark Of The Covenant". The land was purchased from the Hackensack Indians. By the mid 1700's new immigrants broke the Puritan theocracy and the name was shortened. On November 11, 1776 Washington retreated across New Jersey into Morristown, safely 20 miles west of Newark. In 1777 the British camped on Main Street, Orange one mile west of Newark. The Americans and British played tag all across New Jersey for much of the Revolution. On June 23, 1780 they fought the Battle of Springfield, 3 miles southwest of Newark. Newark never took a direct hit and it was the oldest and largest city in New Jersey.

Newark's real growth from an agrarian economy came in the early 1800's when leather manufacturing took off and nearly 90% of the nations leather was produced there. A canal connected Newark to strategic shipping routes and then a railroad replaced the canal. By the mid 1800's manufacturing was diverse and intensifying. The population exploded after the German revolution of 1848 when Irish and German immigrants poured in. The Germans brought breweries, electroplating and diverse manufacturing. The insurance industry moved in.

By 1880 Newark's population was 136,500. In 1890 it was 181,830 and by 1910 it was 347,000. Newark had become the manufacturing, retail and office center for the region. By 1922 it had 63 live theaters, 46 movie theaters and an active night life. Broad and Market Streets was the busiest intersection in the United States.

My grandfather on my father's side was one of those German immigrants. He was a musician who played piano and organ in the theaters. After performing he would steer his horse west and travel up Northfield Road to Livingston where he kept the family house. Unknown to him, he was setting the pattern for Newark's descent by commuting. Just after WWII the population stood at 450,000. Immigrants from Eastern Europe came in and the City took on the flavor of ethnic neighborhoods. I never knew my grandfather. My father found him sitting in his chair, dead, early Sunday morning. His pipe was still warm and he was in the clothes he had worn to play organ in a Newark theater that night.

Before WWII signs of economic decay were well under way. The infrastructure, particularly housing, was in bad shape. What really started to bring Newark down was the flight of the working middle class to the suburbs. The sleepy town my Grandfather rode home to after work was now only a half hour away by car. The State built the Turnpike to take commuters North to South and Route 78 and a widened Route 10 to take them East to West.

Then the tax base declined with aging and fleeing manufacturing. The Federal Government helped out by having the Federal Housing Administration "redline" Newark and pour mortgage money into the safer suburbs. The Feds also provided tax incentives to have industry build new in the suburbs instead of rehabilitating their Newark facilities. Then, while other cities in the Nation were skeptical of building public housing projects and putting poor people in housing projects, Newark gladly accepted the Feds paying 100% of the cost. Newark ended up with a higher percentage of its residents in public housing than any other city in America. Genius: Provide incentives for workers to move to the suburbs and take their factories with them. Build stacked hamster cages to house the locals and drive out the remaining tax payers. The population of working whites was largely replaced by blacks from the South who came there looking for work that did not exist. By 1966 Newark was majority black.

All during the time Newark housing was crumbling there was still ample reason to go there for work. Prudential and Mutual Benefit built new offices. Rutgers University, New Jersey Institute of Technology and Seton Hall University expanded their presence. Newark Airport expanded and Port Newark became the first container ship port in the country. My father had his job of 20 years at a machine shop on Academy Street in Newark and came home to West Orange every night. Ironically, his nickname was "Whitey". Been that way since his hair turned white during the WWII and the guys he worked with and the guys at hunting camp and the scouts all called him that.

My mother's father, Grandpa to me, kept his store on Springfield Avenue. That side of the family was some of the earliest English and Scotch immigrants to the U.S. The earliest was a pensioner who fought for the British in the French and Indian War. He settled in Cold Stream, Kentucky before Daniel Boone. His son's moved north over the line into Ohio and that is where Grandpa was born. Grandpa was moved to New Jersey by his father and so he was the second generation to own the store. I could have been the 4th generation. I worked it when I was a kid and I stocked shelves. In high school I worked the counter when I wasn't life guarding or playing hockey. My mother kept the books and inventory. Grandpa, Mom and Gene who had been with them since the end of WWIl, kept it open 7 days a week. Springfield Avenue was a shopping mecca.

The decline started. Fewer and fewer of Grandpa's white customers came down anymore. They shopped over the mountain in the suburbs where they lived. They went right by if they were still commuting to Newark. It was a matter of convenience. Grandpa changed inventory and now catered to a poorer clientele. Many of his friend shop owners stayed too, but many closed up and moved on. He had owned the building for years and worked it with he and Mom. Overhead was low and so he stayed. By the time I hit high school there was a spiral book behind the counter. It was a ledger of those who owed him money. If he knew them as regular customers he often gave them what they needed on credit.

There were black owned stores popping up. I knew a kid across the street and down the block named "Sweets". He was about 250lbs and played down lineman for Orange High School. His father owned an old fashioned soda fountain with a black and white tiled floor and a counter with swivel stools. Mabel was a hoot. She was a large black woman who always had a too small white "soda jerk" hat perched on top of a whole lot of jet black hair. She never failed to provide us with "egg creams" and talked jokes to us the whole time she was making them. There is no egg or cream in egg creams and I have no idea how they got their name. But Mabel jerked the handles on the long goosenecks that rose from the counter, mixing the perfect blend of our favorite drink. Hence the term "soda jerk". Sweets and I spent a lot of time talking sports. He was going to try to play football after high school. He could have made it. He was a pure athlete in spite of his size. Don't know if he ever did.

Father James was on the street. The mission he served at was on the other side of the street between Sweet's place and our store. He cooked the food that was free to anyone who wanted it. The mission subsisted on whatever anyone could or would leave in a box on the counter and contributions from anyone else the missionaries could hit up. There was a lot of support from the people with money on the other side of the mountain. Most of the store owners kicked in something. Father and I were still close. He was always in a hurry but we at least waved at each other if we didn't talk. Father loved egg cremes as much as I did and the mission was closer to Sweets than I was. Most of the volunteers at the mission were college kids. Seton Hall was right up the road. Upsala was close by in East Orange and Caldwell College was about ten miles away. In 1967 things started to get ugly.

I returned from college the end of May, making the 1,100 mile trip, but also making the mental transition from Midwest to East Coast. My life guarding job was waiting and there was always work at Grandpa's store. When I pulled into the driveway at 1:00 in the afternoon I was surprised to see my father's car. He should have been out on the road ramrodding the outside jobs for the shop. I walked in and he was watching the start of the Yankee game on channel 9.

"Hey Pop!"

He got up, gave me a hug and I felt as though I were holding a bag of bones. Between Christmas break and now, 148 days, he must have lost 10 pounds off of his normal 160. As he stepped back to look at me I saw stooped shoulders and an unsteadiness that was hard to believe. The guy who could go through the woods all day looked like he hadn't been out of the house in a week.

"Glad you're home. I've got something to tell you, come on and sit down."

As he turned off the T.V. he anticipated my next question:

"I know I look like hell. There's been some changes."

I sat and listened as he told me he no longer had a job. He had known Newark for his whole life. When he was a kid he trapped muskrat and fox along Northfield Road, now Route 10, and took the pelts to a tanner down Newark. His father took him to the theaters he played in and Pop would be exposed to the culture of the day. His father had a youth band he organized and he took the kids to every parade Newark and the Oranges had, mentoring anyone who wanted to play an instrument.

After WWII, his father was dead and Pop returned, discharged at the age of 36. He needed a job. He found it at the machine shop on Academy Street in Newark. From 1946 until 1967 he had driven the few miles down the mountain into Newark and helped turn a three man business into one of the largest equipment installers on the East Coast. The shop employed 19 men, all skilled craftsman, who could fabricate anything from a block of metal. Pop worked his way up to Field Supervisor running the outside jobs. The field crews came and went according to how big the job was. I would guess they numbered another 20 skilled men.

I knew how trusted he was by the two brothers who owned the company. No way this man lost his job. I saw the hurt in his eyes as he continued.

"Things changed right after you left to go back to school. We began to see some new faces hanging around. The diner down the block got held up at eleven in the morning and we all started to lock our cars. We came in Monday morning and the place was cleaned out. Anything not nailed down was gone. For Christ's sake, we all lost our tools."

This was not a small thing for skilled craftsman. It took years to find or fabricate the exact tool needed for a particular job. These guys didn't gain experience in a year or two. They invested their lives in a trade and Pop's company grew because they did the job right.

Pop continued:
"The brothers put up the money to replace the guy's personal tools and went out and got the fabricating equipment we needed. They put in a german shepherd who lived in the place 24/7 and a new gate and grates on the windows. Everything got double padlocked. It was o.k. for a few weeks, but I think the bastards were just waiting until they could hit us again. I went to work 4 weeks later, same deal except they had put a bullet into the dog and he was dead on the floor. We all got called in and the brothers told us they were shutting down. I can't blame them. They were sixty something."

My Pop was 58, out of work, and tired. He had worked his whole life.

He was a tough son of a German immigrant. He was taught that you took advantage of the opportunities given you and you made something of yourself. We had a decent house in a nice neighborhood because he worked his ass off. So did my mother. He had always been there for me. He taught me how to handle myself in the woods and how to shoot when the rifle was as big as I was. He organized the Boy Scout troop and he, Sarge and men like them, made us into men. When Hitler took Germany on a path to world domination, Pop, the son of a German immigrant, took up arms as did his brother and they fought for the U.S., their country. I knew how he hurt and I knew why he hurt. He didn't hurt because he no longer had a job. And he wasn't scared. None of the values he had passed on, none of the sacrifices he made could protect us from the sociopaths who were taking over Newark.

There is a certain percentage of mankind that is sociopathic. That percentage doesn't give a damn about anyone else. At the first level they are fairly benign and not cruel, just users. It is all about them. They lack the empathy to feel what they do to others. Out of that group of sociopaths there is a subset that is more ruthless. They look at everyone as potential prey and they don't care if they steal an old lady's retirement money or a car that a kid saved up his whole life to buy. The third subset is subhuman. They lack the basic trait that makes them human beings. They do not value human life. Those who are NOT sociopaths sometimes make the mistake of thinking that these people can be rehabilitated or educated, or changed or that they are somehow victims and owed something by society. Fools.

"Did you go on unemployment Pop?"

"I am not standing in line with a bunch of people who don't want to work. I'll file for social security in a couple of years. I paid into it and they owe it to me. I have my pension from the Union. Your Mom stashed her money and we lived off mine. This house is paid off and we don't need much."

I thought about how we were going to make it and I thought about the last two years of college. I didn't know what the hell I was going to do with my life and I questioned whether it was worth it to continue in school. I offered up a partial solution. "I've got two guys on the swim team who want to get an apartment off campus. That's cheaper than living on campus. I got offered a job to coach at the 'Y' and teach scuba and I'll take it."

Pop went on, "Things are getting rough for Grandpa, too. Gene retired. I won't let your mother drive down to the store alone. Either she goes with him or I take her. I put your double barrel 12 gauge in his office. I go down with him to open and I go back and close him up." "What the hell is happening?" I asked him.

"It's changing. Preacher sees it too."

Pop's dearest friend, "Preacher" was a hell of a guy. He had pitched in the Dodgers organization and might have made it big time if it weren't for WWII. When he got back he was too old. He showed me how to throw a curve ball and I never saw him not smile. He worked at Prudential, made a good living and had a beautiful middle-class home on the East Orange/ Newark line close to Upsala College. Preacher's neighborhood was changing. After the first black family moved in others followed and his street was split about 50/50 white and black. The houses were all kept up. All the black kids knew Preacher and he taught them how to play baseball and throw the curveball. If their dad's weren't home from work yet and he was, they went to him to fix their bikes or blow up a football. Their parents didn't want to live in downtown Newark either. Preacher was a few years older than my Pop. He had retired by this time and could move where he wanted to. He stayed. He liked the neighborhood and the neighbors liked him. He was glad he didn't go down to the "Pru" anymore. The bus ride was becoming a problem for anyone white. He saw groups of young black men he hadn't seen before and they made an effort to intimidate him. Purses got stolen, people got roughed up and if you were white, you drove a car on some streets at your own risk. If you caught a red light you could be in trouble. There were a lot of locals standing around, they had nothing else to do.

Not all areas of the city were bad. The Italians still held "Down Neck" and the North Ward. Middle class blacks bought up houses in the better areas. The center city became more of a hell hole each day as people stacked on top of each other, with no way to make a living, approached a hot summer.

Pop asked me to go down and pick up Mom and follow Grandpa out. I took his station wagon and left my Austin Healey in the driveway. I had seen that car for sale by a guy my father knew and coveted it from the time I saw it. It was a black convertible with a deep red interior and wire wheels. It had some rust spots, but it ran like a dream. I had enough money saved up to buy it and the Chevy that took me coast to coast was on its last legs. Pop wouldn't let me drive the Healey until he took it to the shop and put in a roll bar. The first time I drove it to school I stopped at the top of a hill in Illinois looking at an infinate stretch of straight black top. I put the pedal to the floor, shifted up through the gears and hit the electric overdrive button on the dash when the speedometer hit 120. The tach dropped a couple of hundred RPM and she just kept on. I chickened doing 140mph with my ass 12' off the black top.

As I drove down South Orange Avenue in the station wagon I saw little different. I pulled behind the store into the little parking area that was big enough to hold 3 cars. Grandpa's property backed up to the cement back wall of the building behind it. I walked in and Mom and Grandpa took turns hugging me and there was happiness. Grandpa put the lock on the front door and turned the sign to "closed". We went into his small office and he was reluctant, but he laid it all out for me. I think it wasn't that he didn't want to tell me what was going on, but I don't think he wanted to face the fact that this, what had been his whole life, was about over.

"You know my regulars stopped coming down here. You helped make the changes to inventory. I've still got some of the old locals and I carry some of the new ones I can trust on credit. But there are less and less of them too. We're still making money but I don't enjoy it like I used to. I don't want your Mom coming down here anymore. I am seeing young guys I have never seen before and they travel in packs. Sweets doesn't come over anymore and I heard a couple of the new guys walked into the Mission and took the donation box right off the counter."

"Is Father James still there?"

"I see him, but he doesn't come over here."

My mother just sat and listened. She was never shy about telling Grandpa what to do, but she just sat kind of deflated as he spoke.

Grandpa went on, "I am about ready to retire anyway, but I was hoping your Mom would have an income as long as she wanted to keep it going, at least until you got out of college."

Mom spoke about Pop.
"He doesn't want me to come down here anymore. But I am more worried about him. He can't get another job at his age. It isn't the money. His pension and social security and my social security will give us more than we need. But he sits around all day and watches TV and he is drinking."

I could see that and when he hugged me I felt his chest and neck heave with every breath he tried to take. Years of hard work and smoking were taking him down.

So the three of us devised our plan: I would drive Grandpa to work every morning before I headed for the club to guard. I would pick him up every evening when he closed and we would be out and over the mountain before dark. He would nose it around that he wanted to sell out and see if we couldn't come up with a buyer before I went back to school. He agreed that there shouldn't be any more sales on store credit and he would try to collect what he was owed. He owned the building and so that would go too. He did not want to be a landlord in a town that no longer wanted him. Who needed that when you were in your 70's?

I drove them home and while Pop put food on the table I called Father James even though I had left Illinois 30 hours ago and was wearing out. We talked and he gladly wanted to meet and catch up and he would come to the store after he finished at the mission at 5 tomorrow. I had grown up a whole lot in one afternoon.

I passed out on my bed in the same room I had since I was 5 years old. Seemed to be the only thing still the same in my life.

The next morning I did as we discussed. I headed for the club after dropping off Grandpa. I got there early, signed in with the Manager and headed for the pool. The club was a magnificent 18 holes of golf set on the precipice of the first Orange Mountain with a clear view all the way to New York City. You teed off West, down hill, away from the top of the mountain and lost yourself in the trees around the dense woods. You made the turn at the bottom and teed off back up the hill, climbing until the skyscrapers of Manhattan appeared as you crested the top. The green sat next to the sheer cliff that, at one time, had been the route of the tram that brought 19th century revelers up the mountain to the lake. There was a similar, but larger amusement lake north, across the top of the mountain at Eagle Rock. In the late 1800's and early 1900's people came up the few miles to escape the city.

I went up the ladder of the 3 meter diving board. I stretched out on the board and felt as though I was hovering. The view was unobstructed, straight over the West Orange Valley, Orange, East Orange, and Newark, across the river into New York. The Empire State Building poked the sky and the spire appeared to be eye level from me. This was most beautiful at night. I found beauty in how the stars in the sky met the lights of the city. I did this often and it was my place of tranquility where I could dream. Now I looked and the beauty was gone. I saw it clearly in the light of day, a city that had been born, grew old and was now dying. I saw into it's soul and the last light was going out.

Father James told me he saw it too, but he didn't want to admit it. More poverty and desperate people meant more opportunity for service for him. The college kids had stopped coming to the Mission to help. A couple of teenagers cornered one of the girls against a store front, lifted her skirt and laughed like hell. Who needed that crap? Father doubled down. He increased his hours there and he tried to recruit the locals to help out. He told me that didn't work. They wouldn't work with the whites who were trying to keep it going and the poor wretches who came there to eat didn't want to do anything.

He told me a big dude wearing a huge gold cross on a heavy gold chain approached him. He introduced himself as Bishop Noah. He was nice at first and told Father that he could make it easy for him. He would take over the Mission and turn it into a storefront church and Father could work there as long as he wanted. Father tried to discuss his theology with him, how did he serve the Lord? The conversation didn't go that way. He came back again and basically told Father that he needed to turn it over to him and get out. Yes, two black teenagers had walked in, went straight to the counter and lifted the cash box. None of the 20 or so people eating said anything or did anything. The two walked out just as though they were picking up a food order to go. A couple of days later they came back and did the same thing again.

So ended May 1967.

WINDS OF CHANGE
Eric Burden and The Animals

IN THE GHETTO
Mac Davis/Elvis Presley

Martin Luther King marched from Selma to Montgomery March 25, 1965. I found out when I came home that May that the Reverend Doctor Gerry Mills of the St. Cloud Presbyterian Church had been there with him. The Polish Jew who accepted Christ, Presbyterian Christian minister from the North had marched with the Reverend Doctor Martin Luther King. He told me of the uproar he created with our church when he wanted to go with the group of educators and clergy from West Orange. This was all peripheral to my life until he spoke about it. Sure I read of the March, but it was distant. In New Jersey I didn't see discrimination. I had been raised to accept everyone as a person. I took guys like Sweets as just friends, nothing more, nothing less. In rural Illinois it was even less benign. We didn't have a lot of blacks where I went to college, but those who were there weren't treated any differently then anyone else as far as I knew and I interacted with a couple of them on a daily basis. I ended up singing in a cover band. Our drummer was a local black kid enrolled in the College. He doubled as drummer in a soul band, eleven guys, swinging horn section and all. I'd be playing a place and in would walk five or six of the brothers from the soul group to watch us play. If they were playing and we weren't, I would go to the club where they were playing and watch them. They called me on stage and I called them up and we were musicians. Then we had a beer together. A few weekends I went to Chicago with some of the guys. We hung out at the Rush Street bars and I didn't know there was an inner city.

Dr. Mills told me how he boarded a plane at Newark Airport and flew to Montgomery to meet the march as it ended. He was bused to the parade route and they walked to the steps of the capital to hear Dr. King. Gerry sees things with great clarity. He recalled for me how he noticed the front facade of the building was a beautiful stone but the sides of the building were plaster. He told of how he was advised the march might be rough, particularly because he was white. As they walked toward the Capital they were herded onto the sidewalk by white motorcycle cops who tore up and down inches from the curb. He was heckled by the employees on the second floor of a car dealership, hanging out the windows over his head. He remembered what he had been told before he came down: There will be gray 4 door sedans along the route. These are Federal officers. If things got really bad he was to kick the side of one so that he would be arrested by a Fed not a local. He came back having seen first hand what segregation looked like. The Southern politicians had stalled the Civil Rights Act and Voting Rights Act in '64 and '65 as long as they could, but in the end they failed and Dr. King was on a roll. President Johnson gets much credit for supporting the passage of those Acts and he was a friend to Dr. King, as were many whites. The Acts could not have passed without white support.

I have a long time friend who often sums things up by saying, "Do good and create evil." Some say, "Best intentions go astray." I would say, "Good intentions start noble causes which then get hijacked by people who see opportunity to enrich themselves."

Just over the hill from where I lived in West Orange was the estate of "Richie the Boot" Boiardo. We all knew not to walk out of the woods onto the back of his property. We all recognized the front gate posts with the two curious figurines at the top that marked the personal domain of the gang lord from the era of Prohibition. Prohibition started with good, if somewhat misguided intentions, and guys like Boiardo saw it as opportunity. They turned it into a cash cow for organized crime and the tradition continued with his son, "Tony Boy". The labor unions became the mobs major source of revenue after Prohibition ended. When Newark's government finally got busted, the courts noted that it was more responsive to organized crime than to the people.

The last white Mayor of Newark was Hugh Addonizio. He should have been the poster child for someone capable of turning the city around or at least keeping it from blowing up. He came from humble beginnings in Newark and was a high school quarterback who went on to Fordham University. He enlisted in the army and returned home with the Bronze Star medal. He was elected a Congressman and served in Washington from 1948 to 1962. Then he won his first term as Newark's Mayor. He ran again in 1966 and won. The legal pursuit of corruption in the unions and government did not catch up with Addonizio until 1969, two years after the riots. He was tried and sentenced to 10 years. The Governor, Richard Hughes, had appointed a blue ribbon commission to study the causes of the uprising. They found a "pervasive feeling" that everything in Newark government was for sale. Vultures were picking clean the bones of a city that wasn't dead yet.

- Newark's poison was brewed. All it needed was some stirring and the death of the "Queen City" was inevitable.
- Newark's infrastructure was aging and needed upgrading.
- Federal policy made building new manufacturing facilities out of the city profitable.
- Southern blacks moved in looking for work where there wasn't any.
- The Federal Government's policies kept home mortgage money out of the City.
- The Federal Government's policies sent mortgage money to the suburbs.
- The State constructed new roads making it easy for those with cars to commute.
- Newark welcomed Federal money that built the housing projects people with no work stayed. Why wouldn't they?
- Federal and State welfare programs housed and fed them.
- The inner city was created.
- Working blacks moved out of the inner city to other sections.
- Working whites moved to the suburbs or kept control of their own Newark neighborhoods.
- Newark's infrastructure was collapsing and there was no new private investment.
- The City was losing income and the finances were a mess.
- Crooked government sold to the highest bidders who picked the last meat off the carcass.
- The City waited for someone to harness the hopelessness of the inner city for their own purpose.
- Summer heat was coming.

SUMMER IN THE CITY

The Lovin Spoonful

I don't think there is any kid who has not heard from a grandparent how revolutionary television was for the American family. We grew up on television heroes of the old west like Paladin, The Rifleman, Roy Rogers and Dale Evans and Gene Autry. Davy Crockett died a hero at the Alamo and the Lone Ranger did in the evil doers with Tonto. Vaudevillians made the switch from stage to screen and some of the greatest comics in the world were now available to anyone who wanted to watch. Red Skelton, Milton Burl, Bob Hope and Amos and Andy made the transition and spawned a new crop of entertainers who grew up with television. Lucy, Carol Burnett, Laugh In, The Smothers Brothers added an edge to TV and the medium became the source of news and opinion. In grammar school we loved getting out of class to watch Walter Cronkite bring us history in a series called "You Are There". Families gathered around the small black and white screens to watch the news and entertainment. It was not lost on Dr. Mills that the Sunday night youth group was going to be no-shows the night the Beatles first performed for America on the Ed Sullivan Show. He brought a TV into the community hall and watched with us. TV had it's standards and Ed showed Elvis Presley only from the waist up. The News was news. If you wanted opinion you watched Meet The Press on Sunday mornings. Three then four networks and channels 9 and 11 were all we had. Families adjusted dog ear antennas on top of the TV set if they didn't have an outside antenna. We watched and we believed.

I was fascinated by Reverend Ike. I stumbled upon him streaming to me on either 9 or 11 from his church next to the bridge leading into New York. You couldn't miss the "Blessing Tower" that he designed to be a beacon for those coming to him to be saved. Ike wore immaculate tailored suits in colors of aqua and red. I had never seen clothes like that before and he made a great appearance with full, slicked back black hair. When he sat down on the chair/throne in the center of the stage a crown embroidered on the back rest appeared on the top of his head. I realize now he was one of the first "prosperity gospel" preachers.

What I heard from him was the same values I had been brought up with. I remember one show that went something like this:
He greeted a beautifully dressed black couple who he called to the stage. He walked right past the husband and straight for the wife. He turned to the husband:

"Is this fox your wife?"

The husband nodded and smiled.

"My, you are a fox! And we all know fox is expensive!"

She smiled as he held her hand. Now his attention went to the husband who he called over.

"Tell me, how can you afford such an attractive lady?"

"Well Reverend, I drove a truck to make a living. One day I said to myself, if I can drive a truck, why can't I own a truck?"

"And how many trucks do you own now?"

"I own ten of them. I don't drive them anymore, I let my drivers do that and I take care of the office."

"And how did you get all those trucks?"

"Why I got your "Blessing Plan" and I read it every day and I got the strength to do it myself."

Cut to Reverend Ike holding up a box of cards that were available for a ridiculously low price or maybe they were free, I don't remember.

Reverend Ike continued, "When I want God to bless me I don't ask him to send me money! I ask God to give me the strength to get out there and get what I want! Get off your butts and go get what you want! Get my "Blessing Plan", read a card every morning and keep that thought in your head. Ask God to give you the strength to succeed!"

He held up some of the cards and I saw, what I would now recognize as the basic message of, "The Power of Positive Thinking". Thank you Norman Vincent Peale.

Bishop Noah wasn't a Reverend Ike and he had no interest in taking over Father Jame's Mission so that he could help the poor transform their lives. He saw opportunity. Opportunity to make a profit off the donations that kept the Mission afloat. People with no hope are ripe for the picking and a hundred Bishop Noah's in a hundred store fronts sucked the life out of the mainstream churches.

The second week of June I got a call from Father.

"I can't go there anymore. I went to open yesterday and as I was putting the key in the door I got hit from behind. All I know is that I was on the ground and they kicked me and kicked me. All those poor people who only want food and I can't help anymore."

"Are you O.K.?"

His voice was more sadness than anything else. "Yeah, my ribs are beat up, but I'll be o.k."

"Is there anything I can do, anything you want from there."

"No, I just walked away. I'll find something else. How could they do it, why did they do it?"

If there was someone more intent on helping the poor blacks in Newark I don't know who it was. The mainstream clergy with mainstream churches and mainstream religion helped the community too. There were other food pantries and other outreach programs, but predators were popping up on every corner.

We altered our plan to get Grandpa out. We no longer left the 12 gauge in his office, we carried it with us. There had been too many break-ins along the Avenue although we hadn't been hit yet. I now took him down in Pop's car with the twelve gauge in a case in the back seat. It is impossible for a civilian to get a carry permit for a handgun in the State of New Jersey. True now, truer then. But I said, "fuck it", when I was going down there. The Colt Combat Commander in 9mm was in a shoulder holster under my left arm, covered by my unbuttoned shirt. No way would I belt carry because we were most likely to run into trouble while driving. Getting a pistol off your belt while in a seated position is just too cumbersome.

That June morning I parked in front of the front door of Grandpa's store. We no longer went in through the back because that was basically a trap, blind from the street and surrounded by concrete walls. The only reason I wasn't trying to talk Grandpa out of going at all was because he had a guy from South Orange who owned a bunch of store fronts and low rise apartments, ready to buy him out. Grandpa would get the wholesale value of inventory and about half of what the building would have been worth 10 years ago, but, he would be out and he would have a few more bucks to retire on. We had to hold out until August 1st.

I learned the term "situational awareness" later in life, but I always knew I had it before I knew what to call it. I have always been acutely aware of whats going on around me. When something opens my nostrils or shoots my adrenaline, I see things in microseconds and process things much more quickly than when I am just walking around. In tense situations time slows for me.

As soon as I turned the key and opened the door I was acutely aware of a presence that wasn't ours. I got out the Colt smooth, and as I pushed it forward a black kid holding my mother's cloth coat and a desk calculator emerged from Grandpa's office into the hall. He was 10 feet in front of me and just stared, frozen like he was a mannequin. Thoughts rushed through my head in nanoseconds. I evaluated the situation, saw no physical threat and decided that there was no way I was going to shoot that poor son of a bitch over a cloth coat and a $15 calculator. I told him to go out the way he came in. His expression never changed. He turned and bolted for the back door still carrying what he had stolen. I let him go. The wooden back door was a mess. The pry bar he used to get in was still in the hall.

My father had a hunting buddy, Eddie, from the shop who was still out of work. One phone call and Grandpa did not work there without a gun guarding his back anytime he was in the building. Hell of a way to make a living.

There are many theories as to what touched off Newark that summer. There is one certainty. The inner city had guns. Russell Sackett, a reporter with LIFE MAGAZINE, said that there were meetings between reporters and organized groups of those intent on violence. The non-violent movement of Martin Luther King and others like him was being hijacked. The Revolution Action Movement, US (the Swahili speaking group from Los Angeles), The Deacons for Defense and Justice, The Black Nationalists, Black Muslims, Black Panthers were reportedly in the city.

I got a call at the club the morning of July 13th. Can't forget it, July 13th is my birthday. It was Grandpa telling me that Eddie the guard, was driving him home, that he was locking the door and was closed until things blew over. Crawford, one of Grandpa's oldest customers had come in, paid him the $5.80 cents he had on the books and told him to get out of town now before the city blew up in his face. Eddie wouldn't let Grandpa stay.

On July 12th the police had arrested a cab driver for driving recklessly with a revoked license and took him to the precinct house after he was roughed up. Word circulated in the black community that he had died in custody. They didn't know that he had been taken to the hospital for treatment. A small crowd gathered and stoned the precinct building but there was no real damage of significance. The truth about the cab driver being o.k. never came out. Those in the New York metropolitan area saw violence in Newark on the evening news. It didn't matter that this incident was isolated and small, that no one in the crowd or police was hurt. The TV audience was shown a crowd, rocks being thrown and fire.

The nightly news created a much bigger story than it was at the time and where else was the audience going to get the details in real time?

The damage was done and those waiting for opportunity had it. Grandpa had gotten out in time thanks to Crawford.

By the night of July 13th the stories of violence were pouring in. Fires raged and looting was everywhere. It really hit the fan when the snipers came out. Firemen trying to put out the fires in the neighborhoods occupied by the black inner city had bricks and cement blocks thrown off roofs at them. Then they came under sniper fire. Detective Frederick W. Toto was killed. Fire Captain Michael Moran was killed. At our home in West Orange our doorbell rang and Pop opened it to a big guy wearing a uniform. I don't know what uniform it was, he never came in and it was dark. Pop told me to go get his hunting rifle which I did. He gave it to this guy. It was being reported on the news that Governor Hughes had declared, "They are either citizens of America or criminals who would shoot down a fire captain in the back and then depend on people to speak in platitudes." He called out the National Guard. The Mayor, Addonizio, who still had his reputation intact at this point, saw it all go down the drain.

When it was over so was Newark. 26 were killed, 1,500 were wounded. Of the 1,600 arrested 662 had criminal records.

Pop got the rifle back. To this day I hunt with it. Every time I pick it up I wonder if it killed the sniper who shot the cop or the fireman. I hope it did. Did it kill any of the innocents caught in the crossfire? God, I hope it didn't. The National Guard held the line a block up South Orange Avenue from Grandpa's. When the violence ended I put Grandpa in the back seat with Father James and I drove with Pop cradling the 12 gauge and me with the Colt. We got to what used to be the store. It was a burned out shell, not a piece of glass left in the front window. While Grandpa looked to his left, Father James looked to the right at the Mission. It was untouched and standing in front was Bishop Noah, his big gold cross hanging down in front of a bright blue suit and matching fedora. There was Sweets standing in front of his untouched shop. He saw us, put his head down and walked inside. Didn't say a word or acknowledge us. Nothing. We drove back up over the mountain and Grandpa said nothing and I never heard him speak of it again. Neither did Father James.

Whoever "they" were, they got what they wanted. Whitey was out, and what did they get? Black middle class families trying to do the right thing were hurt the most. Property values plummeted, the remaining jobs left and the vultures came in. The sociopaths had no one to prey on but their own.

The result was the creation of the most violent culture that has ever existed in America. My heart bleeds for the generations of inner city black kids who have been lost. It took from 1967 to 1970 for the violent crime rate in New Jersey to roughly double. Newark took down East Orange and Orange. Irvington went and so did most of the urban area. By 1970 violent crime doubled again assisted by Camden and Trenton. In 1966 the violent crime rate for New Jersey was 161.9 . In 1990 it was 647, an increase of 400%. If you were a child in the inner city and the drug dealers had the flashiest cars and money, who would you emulate? If there were no jobs and you were not taught the value of education, who would you become? If you were taught that this was all whitey's fault, would you develop self responsibility? If you were taught law enforcement was the enemy and because you existed welfare owed you a living, would you be angry? Now project the culture over 3 generations.

MARVIN GAYE-1971
"What's Goin On"

Mother, mother there's too many of you crying. Brother, brother, brother there's far too many of you dying. You know we've got to find a way to bring some lovin' here today. Father, father, father, we don't need to escalate. You see war is not the answer for only love can conquer hate. You know we've got to find a way to bring some lovin' here today. Picket lines and picket signs don't punish me with brutality. Talk to me so you can see oh, what's going on what's going on Ya, what's going on. In the mean time right on baby right on right on.------------

ICE CUBE-released 2008 "Gangsta Rap Made Me Do It"

------I heard nigga back in 1971-------You niggas know my pyroclastic flow---You looking at the grand wizard, war lord vocal chord so vicious and I don't have to show riches to pull off with some bad bitches and it ain't about chivalry. It's about dope lyrics and delivery. It's about my persona ain't nothing like a man that can do what he wanna ain't nothing like a man that you knew on the corner. See 'em come up and fuck up the owner, see 'em throw up Westside California Nigga I'm hot as Phoenix Arizona I'm Utah I got multiple bitches. It's a new law keep a hold of yo riches. Dumb nigga don't spend it as soon as you get it and recognize I'm a captain and you a lieutenant. I can say what I want to say ain't nothing to it gangsta rap made me do it. I can act like an animal ain't nothing to it gangsta rap made me do it------------

Today the violent crime rate in Newark is 40% of the crime in the entire state of New Jersey. Where are the black role models ending this cycle? Where are the cries of the black community about black on black crime? Perhaps they have that in Mayor Baraka who was elected in 2014. When he took over, Newark ranked third in violent crime in the Nation behind only Detroit and New Orleans. He is an educator who had black men wearing ties greeting students on the first day of school. Take pride in yourself for the right reasons. Get an Education, treasure family values. You go Mr. Mayor.

We were driven out, so the solution for us was to leave. We went over the mountain and looked down, knowing that we were looking on an inner city culture totally foreign to us. That is when we stopped looking at individuals and started looking at stereotypes. Is it wrong to be on guard until we get to know the individual? If we have a good heart, aren't we really hoping to separate the individual from the stereotype? Who created the stereotype?

One person not going back to Newark was Grounhawg. With all the stuff I had going on I hadn't seen Rocco all summer. I called his shop, went down and sat around over beers for a while. It had taken Rocco close to a year to find out Grounhawg's name was Calvin. His mother named him after Calvin Coolidge, the plain spoken President from Vermont who she read, said something like "America is work." She loved to read and had her Bible and read newspapers whenever she could get her hands on one. Calvin's father died behind a plow in South Carolina when Calvin was three. She was forced into manual labor and worked to keep them in a shack, all the time drilling into him that he could do better, and that reading and writing were a start. As soon as he was old enough he was in the fields too.

Calvin didn't leave South Carolina until his mother died. With what he and his mother had stashed away he was able to make his way to Newark where he believed he could find a job off the fields that had killed his father and mother way to early. He would have been lost in the city except for the fact he was grounded in the belief that he could make his life better and the key was work. He didn't need much because he never had much. He rented the cheapest room he could find, threw his suitcase on the sagging bed and hit the streets looking for work. He walked each day further and further covering the downtown inner city and the old manufacturing areas which were now mostly vacant factories. Same thing, nothing. A week into this he got on a bus and headed into East Orange, Orange and West Orange on Northfield Road. His mother taught him well, "To make money, you gotta go where the money is." He realized that he could not afford a room, pay for a bus and make no money while he looked for a job to the West. He rolled the dice and paid $150 for a station wagon that smoked but ran. He hand painted the windows:

Grounhawg I fix it all,
no job too small
fair prices good work.

He started sleeping in that station wagon behind the rooming house he used to live in, drove into our neighborhood 7 days a week and drove real slow or parked for a while. I guess he thought as long as he had the sign in the window he would not look out of place. He was right because it didn't take long for someone to hire him for something. He did more than he was paid for and he soon never lacked for work. That is how Rocco met him and the rest you already know. When the riots hit he was living in a two room apartment over the workshop/garage/offices of G and R Construction in the West Orange valley behind the Thomas Edison Museum. He was making more money than he ever dreamed of and had the nicest place to live he could ever imagine and a job with a partner who respected him as a man. Calvin would make the short drive to Newark to see the few friends he had met there or to get a meal, but his focus was on his work. Rocco sat him down the day after the rioting stopped and asked him what he thought. "I got no use for that type of people, not ever going down there again." And so, their decision to focus on Ocean County to the south and the explosive growth was easy. The future was to the south and they would ride it.

Karl was MIA Jersey and was only coming back at Christmas at that point to keep his parents happy. I had only seen him a couple of times after we graduated in '64. He was on the Appalachian Trail somewhere south of Killington Peak, still in Vermont, walking north to south when the shit hit the fan in Newark. He didn't need the money so he didn't have to work and summer time New England was his playground. Newark caught up with him too. His father had called in a favor and arranged for him to have a clerkship waiting for him when he graduated law school. The Superior Court Judge was ready to take him on any time. The County court house was on Central Avenue, Newark, on the down slope into downtown. A statue of Abraham Lincoln sat in front looking into the decay. I wonder what Abe would think about what had happened? Karl came to West Orange for 2 days just before the fall semester started. He took one look at the courthouse on Central Avenue and what surrounded it and he wanted to puke.

I had been keeping tabs on Father James in the weeks after July 13th before I left to go back to the Midwest. Every day I sat at the pool looking off the top of the mountain towards New York. I found no joy in it anymore because I knew what I was looking at. I think it was at that time, before I started my Junior year, that I knew I was out of Jersey. Problem was I loved the people and the culture of the Midwest but I had salt water in my veins and that isn't the Mississippi. I caught up with Father and we settled into the couches in my parent's finished basement. I had been told by Pop, at an early age, that if I wanted to drink, do it at home. The bar in the basement was not off limits and as a result drinking was never a big deal for me. I hardly looked at it. This evening was a different story. I had never seen Father take a drink, but that night he did. Pop had finished the basement himself. I didn't help him, I was just a kid, but I remember I watched as he took a blow torch to plywood just long enough to make the grain stand out. That was his finished wall board as cheap as the cheapest plywood he turned into a custom work of art. He put in a small bar. He built a false wall tucked away in the corner and behind it a closet for our hunting clothes and the locked up guns. This basement became the go-to party place for the neighborhood. I don't think he ever gave it a thought that it would be used as a confessional. That night it was.

Today the drug of choice is opioids. In our day it was alcohol. Weed came a year or two later. There are many types of drunks: There is the happy drunk, the sad drunk, the nasty drunk, the quiet drunk, the uninhibited drunk and my personal favorite, the philosophical drunk. The beauty of being a philosophical drunk is that you can resolve world and personal problems simply by debating and fixing them on the spot. Depending on the degree of alcoholic influence, you may or may not take the lesson into tomorrow. The Indians had peyote, we had alcohol.

The conversation started out much as you might expect. It was aided by the bottle of Early Times Bourbon I took down from the bar shelf. It surprised me that Father didn't comment on the fact I poured us two glasses, straight up, no ice, and he was now sipping on one as I spoke. He wanted to know about my college life and I spent probably 10 minutes talking as he listened. I told him about how grueling training with the swim team was. I told him about the band and that we were good but would never go anywhere with it because there were a thousand better and it was all luck whether you made it anyway. I told him about teaching scuba and how I had done a search and rescue in a lake and swam head first into the body lying in a shallow depression in the bottom, his eyes wide open and calm face and how I had never considered what his family would do when I brought him up. I told him I was set on English literature, philosophy and religion and didn't care if it didn't take me anywhere and where was anywhere any way. By now I was on my second glass.

He wanted to know about the girls. Who had I dated, was I serious with anyone?

"No I am not serious. Why would I want to be serious? The one I really want likes bad boys and I am too nice for her. For Christ's sake, I am 19 years old and just beginning to question why one turns me on and another doesn't. How much "like" is natural attraction and how much is them workin it? They can be anybody they want to be. When God gave them kids he gave them something men don't have, a sixth sense and the cunning to keep their cubs safe. Why do you care anyway? You're not interested in them anyway. So tell me, are you gay or neutered or what? You know you can be neutered by having your balls cut off or your brain can do the job."

Holy shit was I getting drunk.

"I apologize, Father."

"You don't have to." He leaned in and looked me right in the eyes talking slow and deliberate like he was really glad to have someone to tell this to. Why do drunks always lean in and look you straight in the eyes like they are about to tell you something so profound the rest of the world can't know of it?

"I want to. I mean I want to---------," he slowed to choose his words. "Look, I am attracted to them. When you saw me pinned against the curtains on stage I was turned on and scared. When Thunder Bunny had me on the car I was turned on."

I was getting way too drunk. "So did you get off?"

Father didn't smile, didn't get mad and didn't stop. He was intent on confessing to me. Oh shit.

"No I didn't get off. I wanted to and I loved looking at her and I loved what she was doing to me but I was strong. I can't let myself do that. There were girls at the Mission, too. I am not stupid and I know when they were trying to turn me on."

O.K., so I was having trouble with this. Did this guy ever laugh? He was so hung up on this issue that the more he internalized and pondered and denied his natural feelings he hung curtains in his brain until he couldn't see how stupid it was and every time he pulled a curtain aside there was another one so nothing changed.

"So you are attracted to women, they are attracted to you, you want a woman but you won't let a woman. Your not a priest yet so where is the problem?"

"The church says as long as I am celibate for two years before I go to seminary I am o.k., but I am a priest in my heart, have been even when I was in high school. My undergraduate studies have taught me that clearly God created man and woman, that is the natural order of things, and that a priest should be able to relate to either sex as a heterosexual man would, but receive the blessing of celibacy which binds me to the Church. Sex is for procreation."

My head was going to explode. I poured us another drink.

"Let me get this straight: You are supposed to relate as a het, hetrosxl, heterosexual, and counsel people in marriage and all kinds of shit never having experienced a relationship between a man and a woman?"

He started to say something but I had him backed into a corner and I was on a roll. In a moment of instant clarity, happens a lot when I am really drunk and think my thoughts are amazing, I determined to become philosophical and, therefore, I sat back and looked at the ceiling.

"Seems to me you have a couple of options", and I made them up as I thought of them:

"We can get you laid. You get off, you can say you had a relationship with a woman and maybe you are satisfied that you tried it out before you swore it off. Simple, but then you didn't really have a relationship at all. You just got laid and sex is only one part of a relationship, so you really didn't learn anymore about women then you knew before you got laid. That is not to say they want you to understand them anyway. You can do the girlfriend thing and you got about a month to do that because you graduate in 2 years and one month and then you want to get to seminary and I know you can't lie. You can try it, like it, screw around the whole time you are a priest and we can laugh about this in ten years while we share tired jokes about how you got leads in the confessional. You can screw around, they know it, you know it, every woman in your parish knows it and you wink a lot and everyone loves you and you are a hypocrite because you worked around the church doctrine to become a priest loved for the way he treats his flock and how well he relates to them. You can become an Episcopal priest and have a woman, marry, don't marry, whatever, but you eliminate the whole sex thing and I think that makes you a better priest. Who says you gotta be all conflicted about this? It all gets back to the man not the doctrine. You can be a great clergy on the local level and do all kinds of good and it isn't about what church is telling you you gotta do, it's about what your heart tells ya you gotta do. We all know clergy are no different than anyone else, there are good ones and bad ones. How come every great idea gets hijacked by someone looking to use it? A freakin' ancient Jew turns the world upside down with a simple message of love, kindness, forgiveness, including the unincluded, tolerance and everyone's worth as an individual. He tries to undo the Temple system that the Romans use to control the people. The system enriched the priests and the government at the expense of the people and so they killed him, of course, because he was challenging their authority. So you tell me why you need all this doctrine bullshit when your heart has you already serving?"

Holy crap, how far off base am I? I turned to look at him. Father was passed out cold, slumped in the comer of the couch where I had been making out with Sharon two night ago.

The riots of '67 helped me develop an attitude that has stuck with me for life. If something doesn't feel right then leave it. This holds true even if I have no idea what I am going to replace it with. I can't live a life of quiet desperation, miserable but afraid to make a move. I didn't know where I was headed but I knew I could never live in the Oranges again. College worked out about the way I expected. I had to work more but it really wasn't work because I liked what I was doing. I picked up another job. One of the graduates opened a coffee house in the basement of the hotel in the center of town and when I wasn't singing with my group I was working the door. I set up my day to end classes by 2 so that I had a break before swim team at 4. That gave me time to eat, study some and be at the club or the YMCA by 7. That went on Monday through Thursday. If we had a home swim meet on Saturday I got Friday night off. If the meet was away I was driving me and 4 other guys in a college owned station wagon to some campus somewhere in either Illinois, Iowa or Wisconsin. Sunday I slept in.

I had been diving every quarry and lake in the Midwest. We dove Table Rock State Park in Missouri not long after the lake was created. I sat on a tree limb, slightly high from the depth, looking up at my buddy spiral out of the silver surface, circling the black tree in his blue trimmed wet suit. Surreal. I descended into a quarry that was no more than a shaft 50 feet across and went down until we stood on the roof of a moonshiner's car ditched during prohibition. Somewhere I have a picture of me sitting in a railroad locomotive, in full diving gear, arm on the window engineer style. We had hiked through the woods, equipment on our backs, until we hit the high rim of a crater 50 feet in the air and looked across cobalt blue water at railroad tracks running off flat ground on the other side. I lay on my back on the bottom of the quarry at Racine, Wisconsin after we chopped a hole in the ice. I dove a wreck in Door County Wisconsin in water so clear and cold that the rope rigging was still attached to the mast since she went down in 1912. We stumbled upon a Norwegian anchor. Early explorers would weave a basket out of tree limbs and fill it with rocks. When they left they simply cut them loose. I touched history when I dove.

I took an opportunity at Spring break '68 that changed my life. I went with one of my dive buddies to Key Largo, Florida where they had just opened John Pennekamp Underwater National Park. We loaded what passed for a trunk in the Austin Healy with clothes and diving gear. We strapped a tent and two scuba tanks to the luggage rack and he wedged his girlfriend into the back seat. The back seat really wasn't a back seat but two indentations in a platform. Impossible for her to sit facing forward if I was driving because I couldn't get behind the wheel unless the seat was all the way back. My buddy spent a thousand miles pushing his seat back so that his knees weren't under his chin anytime his girlfriend's back pain had diminished enough for her to sit cross ways. This game of passenger seat yo-yo worked itself out when the weather got warm enough to put the top down and she could sit upright. 1,400 miles later we tooled across the causeway and into Key Largo, a loaded down sports car, 2 euphoric divers and a girl who probably developed scoliosis in later life but was having a great time at the moment.

We arrived about 3 in the afternoon, couldn't wait for the next day to rent a boat. We put on our wet suits, mask and snorkel and swam for a mangrove island about a half mile out. The sand bottom was 12 feet below us and we passed over a school of 4 foot hammerhead sharks nosing around. I saw my first barracuda. When we got to the mangrove roots there were all kinds of little fish. On the return swim I found a V-8 engine block someone was using as an anchor for a float. Out of each piston hole was a set of feelers and we systematically picked 8 lobsters out of their apartment house. We ate well that night and later we huddled up inside the tent with a flashlight identifying fish in a book we had brought. I discreetly found time away from the tent whenever it became apparent I should make myself scarce and things worked out nice. We spent most nights drinking with the locals at The Caribbean Club where Bogart filmed "Key Largo".

One day it rained and we put the top up and drove to Key West. We had dived up into Marathon, but going into the lower Keys through Islamorada, over the seven mile bridge eventually into Key West was a ride of a lifetime. I knew Henry Flagler had spent a fortune to link mainland Florida to Key West, but you gotta see it to believe it. We drove over the ribbon of road that had been the bed for his railroad. Where he could, he put track over sand and coral. When he ran out of land he poured concrete arches in the water. Many men died in what was then a constantly soggy, mosquito infested jungle. When a hurricane hit they had no where to go and water swept them off the land and they were just gone. Those left got it done. When the railroad was replaced by cars and trucks they simply made two lanes out of his rail bed. There was a lane in each direction just wide enough to allow two cars to pass if you were real careful and there was no guardrail some places and what was supposed to be a guardrail in others. The drive was like being suspended in air with the Gulf of Florida on one side and the ocean on the other. I loved that Cuba was only 90 miles away.

In 1968 Key West was still as wild as any city in the U.S. could be. There were no "posers" like it is today. No one rented a motorcycle so they could look cool. There were no tee shirt shops and no cruise ships. The residents were raw and they liked it that way. If you went to a bar you could be sitting next to a writer or artist or a fishing captain with no teeth and not know who was who. I loved the feeling of freedom and the edge it had. Hell, I think they still had pirates. They did have Tony Tarracino, who, when he ran for Mayor used the slogan, "All you need in life is a tremendous sex drive and a great ego, brains don't mean shit." He won. We stumbled upon Captain Tony's Saloon, met him, found out he was from Elizabeth, New Jersey and I took it as an omen. The money was running out so we did too. I would be back, drawn to the Keys like a lover to a bed.

SUZANNE
Leonard Cohen

The hot summer inner city riots of 1967 shook up a lot of people. When you piled the Vietnam War and the draft on top, it made for a rough couple of years that changed our lives forever. My next door neighbor lives with no legs from the knees down, metal plates holding his bowling wrist together and assorted pieces of fragments from the booby trap he stepped on coming to the surface and poking through his skin 45 years later. I exchange emails with an expatriate buddy who has lived in Mexico since he was discharged in 1970. He comes to the U.S. once a year for his Veteran's Administration medical. They prescribe the same pain killers and mood stabilizers and he goes back home. Another guy I fished with back in Jersey can not sleep unless he has the same 12 gauge shotgun he carried in Nam under his bed. Limits where he can travel.

Every war leaves it's trail of the physically and mentally damaged. Some are in uniform being blown up by others in uniform. Some, whose backyard it gets fought in, get blown up whether they wanted anything to do with it or not. The old men start the wars with their policies and the young men die for them. That assumes the young men buy in.

World War I had literal lines separating opposing armies and they knew who the enemy was. They took turns slaughtering each other while they lived in ditches. The war had started with armies that still relied on horse soldiers and codes of conduct for how to kill each other. It ended with mustard gas, tanks, aircraft and mass slaughter that had no honor. When it was over millions died and I am not sure anyone knew why, other than a royal family member got assassinated in a bizarre twist of fate and interconnected royals in various nations held a grudge. When my mother died at 101 I found a diary her uncle, Grandpa's brother, had kept. He started writing on legal size paper when he boarded the troop ship for England. It is the work of a young man filled with enthusiasm and energy. He wrote as far as the patrols he was doing in the forest in France and not understanding what he was supposed to be doing before he got to the trenches. The center section is missing, damn I wish I had it, but the last pages are him in a hospital waiting to go home. It was written by a tired unemotional man with no energy who just wanted to go home. The dates in the diary show that his whole experience in France was 9 days.

Hitler came out of WWI a trench soldier and courier, bitter for the way France, in victory, stomped on Germany. France left Germany a starving wreck deeply in debt. The victor gets to write the history. Some thought should be given to how and why Hitler became a monster and the role France's brutality in victory played in it. Anyway, President Roosevelt kept the U.S. out WWII for as long as he could until Japan attacked and we had to go in otherwise we would all be speaking German. Everyone at home was needed to support the War effort and they watched the maps of the Allies pushing back the Germans and then the Japanese. Definitive progress, cost in dead and money accepted, national spirit of unity.

Korea set us up for confrontation with Communism. General Mac Arthur lost his job over his strategy for victory in Korea and he was removed. And so we didn't finish it and today that set up a maniac leading North Korea staring across a no man's land at South Korea. Since the armistice of 1953 they are still technically in a state of war even though probably nothing will happen until the North Korean drops an atomic bomb on somebody. But not a lot of U.S. troops died or were maimed compared to other wars. One who wasn't lucky was a good friend of my grandfather who froze to a machine gun at Chosin Reservoir and spent the rest of his life in a bed, with no legs and useless hands, dialing a phone 8 hours a day and working sales to keep his family. First U.S. war that ended without a victory. We were there as a colonial force fighting an ideology, but at least the armies pushed back and forth in measurable miles and with landmarks until the stalemate ended at the 38th parallel and the real stalemate began and exists today. This was our first experiment with containment of an ideology.

Did we learn anything about fighting a colonial war in someone else's country? Hell no! Lets move into Vietnam and continue our policy of containing communism.

The Vietnam War bred cynics the way other wars bred heroes. Eisenhower was a career military man who knew the price he paid in human currency to win WWII. When he left as President he tried to tell Kennedy to stay out but it was Kennedy who escalated it. He propped up a weak South Vietnam government. In 1963 Johnson doubled down and in 1964 The Gulf of Tonkin Resolution was passed and Congress gave the President the right to unilaterally conduct a war. Brilliant. The War began as a civil war begun to remove a corrupt Vietnam government. Ho Chi Min, leading the attack, wanted peace with the U.S. We rejected the offer, our government preferring to prop up weak and corrupt presidents of Vietnam. In 1965 we sent in combat troops. In 1968 the North's push, the Tet Offensive, proved we were not winning.

The politicians could only create the illusion this was a noble effort for just so long. Were we really stopping communism? Were we defending people who couldn't defend themselves? Were we there to expand our colonial sphere of influence? Some reasons were more noble then others. Some held more truth. Many of our fathers bought in. These were the guys who laid it all on the line to win WWII. We were in a war and it was their son's turn to fight. I watched my father's attitude change. He advised me to stay out. Fewer and fewer Americans were buying the crap anymore. Increasingly we did not know who the enemy was and why our friends were dying. This was not an all out effort and a unified national spirit.

This fractured America and tore apart patriotism. Some kids lost their parents because the kids opposed the war and their parent's branded them as cowards or traitors. To this day our generation does not know how to adequately express the difference between reverence and disgust. Reverence is for those who deserve our love and who died physically and emotionally in Vietnam while we stayed home. Disgust is for the politicians who got us into it, didn't want badly enough to end it and were willing to provide a generation for cannon fodder. The poor were more likely to go. Everyone was signed up with Selective Service. But there were educational deferments, occupational deferments, religious deferments and all could be taken advantage of if you had the money. In Karl's case he had it easy. His father made one call to the Judge and Karl would never hear from his draft board again.

By the start of my senior year, 1969, the stink of the war and the distrust of government had gotten too close. There weren't enough young men willing to go to replace the 59,000 or so that would eventually die there. Even in the bastions of conservatism that were the Midwest college campuses, there was a growing awareness that this was all bullshit. In California the "Flower Power" and peace movements were real and spreading. The Grateful Dead, Jefferson Airplane, and a thousand other singers, songwriters and poets turned the tables on government and turned cynicism into active resistance. It hit the Midwest hard in May of 1970 when Kent State happened and the military, on our own soil, blew away some kids protesting the War. 13 seconds, 67 shots, 9 wounded, 4 dead and so was patriotism.

Two years before President Johnson's approval rating had gone from 48% to 36% and he wouldn't run for re-election. Nixon won and began withdrawing American troops to the coast by 1970.

Government deception was the name of the game. They said we were winning. We weren't. They said we weren't going into Cambodia. We were. In 1971 "Pentagon Papers" made public the deception and we were pissed. In 1973 Nixon got our fighting men out, but we propped up a weak South Vietnamese government until the North finally over ran the American Embassy in Saigon on April 29, 1975. Forty years later Vietnam, unified by the communists, is our friend. Go figure. Politicians with power agendas come and go. Ideologies change. 99.9999999999999999% of the people in this world just want a better life for themselves. The world sags under the weight of individuals who seek power and wealth at the expense of the other 99%.

What mattered to us in 1969 was that the real conflict was at home. Our generation was forced to question what we had been taught. We saw that President's lie. Government's lie, and both are more than willing to sacrifice people for the sake of what? We were pawns to be used for increasingly blurred motives of personal ambitions and the seeking of wealth and power by those who are supposed to be motivated to help the people who elected them. Gone were the days of our fathers when Americans believed when your government called for a just war it was one. This was when America fractured into the inner city culture and the rest of society. This was when my generation wrestled with the thought that our parents fought just wars but we were forced to question. America would never be the same. National unity was gone and so was the beginning of the erosion of the values that built a great nation. This began with us then.

On December 1, 1969 we waited for our birth dates to be pulled so that we could be told who would be drafted to replace those dying in Vietnam. Karl didn't care, his father had seen to that and he would never be called. I don't believe for a second that he had any other thought than he would never sacrifice for anything. Father was in the clear. His number was pulled 314 and it was unlikely he would ever be called. I was conflicted. My number came up 42. I was screwed. I had a college deferment until I graduated six months later. Damn if I knew what I was going to do. Part of me felt a sense of guilt if I didn't go. Part of me was still rooted in the idea of the adventure of it even though I no longer believed in it. In January the war came to me and it changed everything.

It was one of the rare week nights I wasn't teaching or coaching and I wanted to make the most of it. I made my way downtown pulling the collar of the rawhide and shearling coat up around my neck, trying to hide from the cold you can only know if you have been in the Midwest in January. The wind drives down from the north with nothing on the flat land to stop it and it is bitter. I wanted change from the apartment with roommates, the swim team and the basement club. The bar I headed for usually had a mix of college students and locals, most of whom were farm hands looking for cheap beer and the chance at maybe breaking the boredom by being around the college kids. I opened the door and headed for the dark wood, life scarred bar that had seen a lot of use for a lot of years. On one end was a jar of pickled eggs that sold for 10 cents. Hamms on draft was 25 cents and if you were short on money this was a good place to be. A lot of the college kids and locals knew me from the basement club and I think they were surprised to see me here alone. I made my way to the corner of the bar where it wrapped around so I didn't have to look at myself in the mirror that ran it's length.

Danny was one of the guys from the swim team I liked the most. Here he came with another guy and there went my night of quiet solitude. He was a sophomore and we had talked often of things other than swimming. He had never been out of the Midwest and I guess the fact I was from the East Coast and had been to Florida made me interesting to him. He introduced me to Vern his older brother. I held out my hand and Vern shook it, not really looking at me as he did. I did get a polite nod. Danny told me Vern was back from Nam and he had brought him across from the family farm in Iowa, outside of Davenport, to spend a few days. Vern was about 5'9", wore black rimmed glasses and couldn't have weighed 160. I muttered something to Vern about being glad he was safe and I did get another nod of acknowledgment. I didn't really know what to say and I didn't want to steer the conversation his way. I would have liked to hear about his experiences over there but judging what I saw he looked like he wanted to get away from his thoughts too. I made it a point to not buy him the first beer.

Danny sat between us and I had a clear look across the corner of the bar at Vern. Danny began to tell Vern about how he rode in the station wagon I drove when we traveled to swim at another college. The first beer kicked in and Danny told him about the time we drove to Northfield, Minnesota. Coach checked us into a motel which happened to be straight across a two lane highway from a bar with a flashing "open" sign. I was rooming with another senior who was also from Jersey. It had been a long drive and when the coach knocked on the door at 9pm for bed check. Chuck and I were still wound up. We let coach go, waited about a half hour, opened the sliding glass doors facing the highway and crossed to the bar. It was Friday night and only ten so what the hell. One thing led to another. Chuck was built like a brick shit house with black hair that started just above his eyebrows and a smile that lit the place up. It wasn't long before he roped in two ladies who turned out to be cheerleaders for the college we were swimming against. He closed the deal and we headed for our motel room about 11. By then it was snowing and there was maybe a half inch on the ground. We partied for an hour and sent them back across to the bar. The next morning Coach got us all up and told us the walk up the street to the restaurant would do us good. He led us around the corner of the entrance to the motel parking lot and up the sidewalk. He never broke stride as he crossed the four sets of footprints in the snow that led from the bar straight to our room and the two sets of small tracks that went back. All he said was, "I am expecting some great times out of you guys today." Chuck set a conference record in the 100 Fly, I faded and ended up second in the 1,000 yard freestyle. Cheerleaders don't go to swim meets.

Vern smiled, I bought a round and pretty soon I was learning all about their farm life in Iowa and they were learning about life around New York City and the Jersey shore. It was clear to me that we could talk about anything and the conversation was easy once Vern knew I got the fact he was here to chill out and relieved I did not ask him about Vietnam. The cowboy that sat down next to Vern was one of those guys trying to be real nice but clueless that the person he was trying to talk to didn't want to talk to him. He heard our conversation and next thing he was into it. Danny tried to suggest he find someone else to talk to, but Cowboy wasn't getting it. Then Cowboy spotted the marine corps ring on Vern. It was on. "So you been to Nam?"

"Yeah just got back", said Vern quietly never looking up. He drained his beer turned away from Cowboy toward us and had the barmaid slap down another one before the conversation could go any further.

I just started to talk. Hell, I don't remember what I was saying, but Vern was looking me in the eyes, smiling and nodding his head and ignoring Cowboy and I knew I was doing good. Danny joined in and we did our best but it wasn't long before Cowboy leaned way in, ignored us and asked Vern, "So I guess you're glad you became a jar head huh? I was Navy myself. Wish I was in now and had a chance to shoot some of those slant eyed bastards. Course I am too old and they wouldn't let me take my 30-30 would they?" His attempt at humor fell short and Vern's expression didn't change.

"You shootin' that M-16? How many you shoot with it?", Cowboy said all eager waiting Vern's response.

Vern started to get up and I could tell from his actions that he was just gonna leave. I walked around him and got between him and Cowboy who was being real nice and Cowboy was leaning around me still trying to talk to Vern. Danny was grabbing their coats and this was taking way too long. Cowboy wasn't shutting up and I guess Vern had had about enough. I felt

Vern put his hand on my shoulder and I turned toward him. He mouthed, "It's o.k. I got this."

He brushed me to the side and his strength amazed me. He leaned forward as though he wanted Cowboy to think this was gonna be special for him to hear. I knew that this was when the guy leaning in would get in the first shot and take out the other guy quick with an upper cut, head butt or use the knife he might have on him and I didn't know anything about Vern other than he was a Marine who served in Vietnam and that I liked him. No worries, Vern talked.

"You wanna know what it's like to shoot someone? You wanna hear all about 'Nam?"

Cowboy's smile widened in anticipation.

"I was a 19 year old kid. I was already tired of the farm and I wanted to see stuff. My father was ready to kill me when I told him I enlisted. By the time I get out of basic we're all indoctrinated about what our job over there is gonna be."

Vern ordered a shot of Jim Beam straight up and dropped it into his beer.

"They fly you over on a big bright commercial jet with stewardesses in tight skirts telling you they'll see you in a year. When you step outside the first thing you smell is burning shit. How do you get rid of the waste from thousands of G.I's, you put it in 55 gallon oil drums, mix it with gasoline and burn it up. They show me where to sleep and the next day I am handed an M-16, boonie clothes and told to get on a helicopter. I am airborne for an hour and I get off and they load 3 blue body bags on. An hour later I am inside two acres of barbed wire with under ground bunkers between sleeping tents and a gate that leads down a dirt road to a little vil where everyone wears black pajamas and straw hats and just wants to work their fields. A sergeant asks who the new guy is, that would be me, and gives me a lecture that's meant to keep everyone else safe. 'Forget anything they told you. We are all just counting the days until our year is up. Don't do anything stupid, in fact don't do anything until I tell you to do it.' I go out on patrol the third day I am there with a bunch of 19 and 20 year olds who have the eyes of old men and they crack jokes about me and they put me in the middle so I don't fuck them up. We carry a hundred pounds of shit on our backs and we walk along the fields and up mountains. For 4 days I am wet, covered in mud and can't sleep because the mosquitoes will carry you away. And what is the point of this? It only takes me one patrol to know that the enemy is only going to be found when they want to be found. Usually they find us with a booby trap that rips the legs off or the guts out of someone I know. So I hated them but they hated me more. All they wanted to do was farm their land. Now the Vietcong regulars go to their village to enlist them and if they don't fight me the Cong hangs and kills someone in their village and now they will try to kill me. So I spend most of my time trying to figure out who is trying to kill me and who isn't but I understand why they want to.

We get back that time and we were lucky. No contact was made and no one stepped on anything to get themselves blown up. I haven't slept more than an hour a night and I drop onto my cot in the same clothes I wore for 4 days. It all goes to shit when we get attacked. The sergeant grabs me and puts me on the perimeter inside the barbed wire. For the next 4 hours I lay flat on the ground, hold the rifle over my head and I empty magazine after magazine over the wire shooting at god knows what in the trees outside our perimeter. It's all explosions, heavy and light weapons and confusion. I see one dark shape inside the wire and I shoot him, the only time I took aim all night. Mortars are coming in and the guy next to me takes a hit that almost cuts him in half and leaves his intestines outside his shirt. I listen to him crying for his mother but that all ends when he dies before the medic can get there. It didn't affect me until after it was all over.

The attack stops before the sun comes up and I can see a couple of bodies in the wire. The son of a bitch I shot is wearing an Ohio State tee shirt and it's the same kid I gave the shirt to when he sold us weed before I went on patrol. He never knew what hit him. I got lucky, the round was a head shot. You wanta know what an M-16 does? He had a small hole under his right eye and the back of his skull and hair was hanging off the wire behind him. I looked at him and puked my guts out. From then on I looked at them in their Vil and they were the same people selling us shit during the day and trying to kill us at night and this was their land and not mine. I knew who his mother was and I don't know how she knew I was the one who killed her son, but every time she saw me she started screaming what I could not understand. After a while I didn't care who I killed because I didn't know who was the enemy and so you just eliminate any threat. I wasn't the new guy anymore and I got it all and I was just like everyone else. I just wanted to live through my year and go home. How do you win a war like this? You don't. The people hate you because all they want is their way of life and because of you they are caught between you killing them or being brutalized by the Vietcong. I didn't want to decide who lived and who died. I didn't want to find out how much of a beast I could be. Some of the guys started using civilians like they were some kind of damn toy. A lot of guys loved the brutality and got into it. I stopped judging them but I didn't do anything to stop them and I saw parts of my soul I didn't want to see. So tell me something, now I am back and what the fuck do I do now because Vietnam followed me home."

Cowboy had stopped smiling long ago. Vern turned to me, shook my hand and looked into my eyes wanting me to understand I was looking at a man who would relive these things again and it would be no better the next time. He wanted me to understand without having to say anything to me and I did. He walked to the door and into the cold and dark without a coat. I trailed him into the night and I let him go. I hung back until he was gone.

FOUR DEAD IN OHIO
Crosby, Stills, Nash and Young

VOLUNTEERS
Jefferson Airplane

SAN FRANCISCO
John Phillips/ Scott McKenzie

BALLAD OF THE GREEN BERET
Barry Sadler

WHERE HAVE ALL THE FLOWERS GONE
Peter, Paul and Mary

Vern sealed the deal for me. I called my mother and Pop to ask them what they thought of me continuing on after graduation with another deferment. Pop, the man's man, World War II veteran, 2nd generation German immigrant, a man who loved this country, told me to do what I had to do to stay out.

I called up the coach at Western Illinois University who had gotten me involved in the diving we were doing. He had been pitching me to go to Miami and start running a dive boat to the Bahamas. I wasn't going to do him any good if I got drafted and that was likely. I asked him if he had any connections in any schools down that way so that I could get a teaching job. He told me he had a friend in Islamorada in the Keys who was principal of a private school. It only took one phone call and I drove nonstop on a long weekend in February of '70 for an interview. He needed a swimming coach and someone to teach marine biology. The fact I could coach track as well sealed the deal. I didn't even ask what it would pay. He told me to take as many education courses as I could over the summer and report to school first week in September. That first year I was paid $7,065 plus another $780 for coaching swimming and track. I figured it out one time and it came to about 75 cents an hour to coach.

I have never been truly lonely. I believe an only child has some advantages and that is one. Moving on was a new adventure. The greatest changes of my life spanned these months. They came at me and I rose with them easily and I found reasons to leave the past behind.

I enrolled in a university close to college and extended the apartment lease for the summer. I didn't go to graduation. Instead I took the five days I had before the start of the summer session and I turned the Healey east to see Mom, Pop and Grandpa. Mom and Pop had a contract on the sale of the West Orange house. Grandpa was already retired in the house on the river in Shoretown and Mom and Pop were going to move in with him. I drove straight there. Have you ever had the experience that you were in a place familiar but you could not picture yourself ever having been there before? What used to be gravel streets were now paved. The pine trees I walked through barefoot as a child to get to the only store on the main road were replaced by houses. The river that had been my solitary play ground was being torn up by the screaming outboard motors of too many boats. I put up with the traffic and drove around the end of the river away from the ocean and came down the other side. I crossed the bridge and headed for the boardwalk. The old bridge I fished and crabbed under was gone, replaced by concrete higher and longer.

Pop was in rough shape and the man was only late 50's. I could see his chest heave with every breath and his lips purse as he sucked in air. God damn cigarettes. Grandpa had always been as physically straight as a ramrod and possessed of a great dignity that simply radiated. Now I saw sadness and great shoulders caving with the weight of the world that used to be collapsing on him. Grandma had died years before and now his work was gone and I felt him joyless in the house on the river. Mom and I talked about it. She saw it all happening and was determined to ride through the changes of a dying father and a sick husband. Some times going home isn't that at all. I was out of time and I left, heading back to the Midwest for the last time.

I returned to the college. Beat from the 18 hour drive, I resolved to have one drink and sleep. I walked into the empty bar at 5 o'clock and was halfway through a beer when Trish walked in.

"Hey lady, what are you doing here?"

"Killing time until I start grad school. Is this place depressing or what? Are you going to buy me a beer?"

She had been dating Gary, one of the guys on the swim team. I always liked her and loved the way she looked. I had never been with her outside of a group. I had watched her then, trying to not let her see that I was. She answered my question before I asked it. Gary had headed for Officer Candidate School. At 21 with it all going for her she wasn't going to be the girl waiting back home.

After 2 beers it came out. I figure women at 21 are about ten years older emotionally then men. At 21 most men are just stupid and slobbering and women understand that and can turn it to their advantage when they want.

"Did you really think I didn't see you looking at me when I was with Gary?"

This could go one of two ways and it was all up to her: Either she was going to bust my chops and have some fun with it or she was looking to scratch the same itch I had. The next day she moved out of the mostly empty sorority house into my apartment. The fact neither one of us wanted to be emotionally available was good because the sex was easy and caring. We could have gone somewhere together but separate roads had been chosen and we knew we could make it last this way for a couple of months and not get hurt. When she rode me to get the feeling she wanted exactly right she looked into my eyes and we both knew that what could have been cheap wasn't.

I locked the apartment door for the last time and neither one of us offered up a way to stay in touch. It only took a minute to reach the straight 4 laner and work up through the gears pointed south. I have never had a feeling of total euphoria like that since. It wasn't about leaving a place I didn't like because I did like it. It was about being able to start totally fresh with changes so great that even though I was only minutes removed the past wasn't even in my rear view mirror. I took the long road to the Keys once I hit Florida, traveling the center part of the state. I traveled on Route 27 to Route 29 through the racing town of Sebring where they had converted an old airfield into a racing venue. I steered the Healey onto the road course and blew around it a couple of times. I turned east through Okeechobee and passed through Lauderdale. Armed with an employment contract I stopped at a Pontiac dealership and traded the Healey for a 1969 GTO. God I loved that car. But now the transition was complete.

CHANGES IN ATTITUDE CHANGES IN LATITUDE

Jimmy Buffet

Back in Jersey Father James was fully focused on beginning his life of service as a priest. I guess the Church policy of being celibate in order to cement a priest to Christ and to the Church was put in place for guys like him. Undistracted, he blew through his undergraduate work in three years and got himself into a seminary. That didn't work out and he transferred to St. Joseph's Seminary in Princeton for the four years he needed to be ordained. There were plenty of opportunities to serve after Newark and that is what he did when he wasn't studying. This was a race against time for him. While Americans wrestled with what Vietnam really was, Father

James saw it as opportunity and he didn't want to miss it. He lucked out. When he graduated the war had another year to run and he wasted no time enlisting as an army chaplain.

His mother had been right. He wasn't like the others and he was glad he had listened to the voice that told him to be close to God and reject the worldly. He no longer felt conflicted about anything. He felt only the compulsion to serve and here were soldiers who needed him. He saw it in their eyes when he served them communion. He was the messenger who brought hope. He was the healer of young minds. He floated somewhere above all that was happening around him and he was consumed by his state of grace.

Father James landed on the coast of Vietnam and was on a helicopter headed to the interior a few hours later. He had never seen so much green as he did looking out the helicopter door as the chopper swung around the mountain and headed for the dirt landing strip of some outpost up by the DMZ. He didn't know the name of the place. Did it really matter? It was like a hundred others where boys sweated out living until their year was up. He descended into the dust and dirt kicked up by the choppers blades as it landed. The flight crew drove out the replacements who were there to replace the bodies in the blue body bags lined up and ready to be loaded for the ride home.

The mortar was hidden in the tree line. The gun crew knew what they were doing. They waited until the chopper was on the ground before sending in the first round that thudded into the dirt 30 yards short. The door gunner pushed Father out and pitched the portable altar box containing the Host and his other supplies after him. The ground troops laid everything they had into the tree line. That didn't stop the next round from taking out the graves registration officer standing next to the blue body bags.

Father walked the few yards to the kid laid out in front of him who was feeling around for his leg that wasn't there anymore.

"Get down you asshole", shouted the lieutenant who was yelling for a medic while trying to fashion a tourniquet from the kid's belt to put around the stump before he bled to death.

Father knelt down, made the sign of the cross in the blood on the kid's forehead, and began the Our Father. The lieutenant slapped the kid's helmet on Father and the kid's blood ran down Father's forehead. Father stood, looking toward the eyes of his God and began his beseeching prayer as the chopper lifted off and the door gunner opened up on the tree line with his 50 cal. The last round the mortar crew got off before they were shredded blew Father off his feet. He was lifted, arms outstretched, palms raised in his beseeching prayer, the kid's helmet blown away and their co-mingled blood running down his forehead. He hit the ground on his back in that position as though God had taken him from the cross and laid him in the dirt between the wheel marks left by the chopper. He didn't move from this communion of body, blood and dirt until they picked him up and placed him on the stretcher with his arms folded across his chest.

He felt no pain. His mind made him all spirit and soul and his body mattered not at all. He was peaceful and all seemed surreal and un-worldly. For years he replayed this and he never got closer to answering his question of whether he had seen God.

From the time Father James jumped to the ground and felt Vietnam under his feet to the time he landed on his back was 37 seconds. They patched him up while they loaded the blue body bags and flew him out with the dead and the graves registration officer missing his right leg.

Nixon got us out of actual combat in Vietnam with The Paris Peace Accord signed January 27,1973 and I stayed teaching at the school until the end of that school year. Those three years cemented me to the Keys. There was so much opportunity for diving, fishing and boating that I decided to leave teaching and see what I could do in business. Pop's sister, my dear Aunt Ruth, lived in Clearwater on Florida's west coast. Mom, Pop and Grandpa came to visit her, returned home, sold everything and retired there too. The whole family became New Jersey expatriates. The South Vietnamese army didn't do too well after we stopped U.S. military operations. In April 29, 1975 the U.S. embassy in Saigon was over run and Vietnam was unified under the communist forces. So what was it all for??????????

WE GOTTA GET OUTTA THIS PLACE
Barry Mann and Cynthia Weil / The Animals

FORTUNATE SON
Creedence Clearwater Revival

PURPLE HAZE
Jimmy Hendrix

Thank you Doug Bradley and all who served. These songs were chosen by you as the songs listened to the most while in 'Nam.
Published November 10, 2015

When I cruised the GTO through Florida City in the fall of 1970 it was the last dry piece of mainland I would see for a while. There was nothing behind me and I was anxious to pass the Last Chance Saloon where US 1 became the causeway cutting off a corner of the Everglades and shooting straight into Key Largo. Key's people identify everything by mile marker. At 107.2 I passed over the Jewfish Creek drawbridge and saw the familiar markers of the Intracoastal Waterway leading under it headed south into Florida Bay. I entered Key Largo. It is possible to take a boat from Manasquan Inlet, 20 miles south of New York City, my inlet as a child, to Key West Florida and never go into the ocean. When leaving Biscayne Bay south of Miami you could take this protected route or stay on the ocean side and the Straights of Florida. If you chose the ocean it wasn't bad in most weather as long as you stayed inside the reef. What makes the Keys such a fishing paradise is the shallow water of Florida Bay and the Everglades on one side of this strip of land and the ocean on the other. There is a huge variety of inshore fish and all you need is a small boat and a good guide. Ocean side the water drops off into the Gulf Stream only a few miles offshore, making it a short run for big game fish. Live aboard boats are anchored and docked on both sides. Some are transient and some are home to locals who dropped anchor and never left.

At 104.2 I pulled into the parking lot of the Caribbean Club where I had dropped my own anchor a few years before. The hotel set where Bogart made "Key Largo" in 1948 was a parking lot, but the dock was still in the same location. The bar was typical of old Key's hang outs. John Pennekamp State Park, where I first dove the Keys, is at 102.8.

In 1970 my world was compressed into an area that spanned the upper to middle Keys, mile markers 104 to about mile marker 70. The width of the Keys varies from maybe a half mile wide in some locations to only yards in others. As you get further toward Key West, there is no land at all, just a concrete ribbon over water of pale greens and blues. The road in those days was that 2 lane ribbon on top of Flagler's railroad bed with little or no guard rails. Going was slow and you paid attention. I went to Key West sometimes, but with teaching, coaching and running dive boats weekends there wasn't much non-local time. Key West was mile marker "0".

When you teach in the Keys you get to know everybody who is local through their kids. I soon knew most of the fishing and diving families and all the local merchants. Some were expatriates from the mainland who came here for a quieter and simpler life. Some came just because of the diving and fishing. All either loved the lifestyle of being a local or they moved on. There was little to do besides live with the water and hit the local watering holes at night.

I have no idea what percentage of teachers marry teachers, but when I started working at school with Jessie I was a gonner. She was a Key's native who grew up around, over and under the water. Jessie was the gym teacher and what started out as coaches having a late drink after work became Jessie crewing the dive boat for me on the weekends and Jessie moving into my place. She was beautiful, athletic, tight, and could shoot a tequila as well as anyone in Key Largo. I believe women have it much tougher than men. They grow up faster because they have to. As long as they are the ones giving birth to children they have a lot of decisions to make that a man in his early 20's doesn't even think about. At least I didn't. I thought with my little head instead of my big one and she was wonderful and exciting and I was intoxicated and so I married her in 1975 encouraged by most of the faculty and locals who thought we were perfect together but who hadn't considered I didn't know shit about married life.

We looked at each other one Sunday morning 7 years later and the fire was gone for me. She knew it. I didn't know what I wanted, I just knew I wasn't happy. She was wise enough to understand more than I did. With no kids and plenty of money and a solid job and nobody mad at anybody and me feeling guilty and horrible, she made the separation and eventual divorce easy for me. I will never fully understand how she must have hurt and what she hid, but each year I get older I feel more of it. As I age I think of things I regret. I didn't know those things then. But I understand now that I lived and that is what living is. I was not always wise and I was not always empathetic and I was sometimes selfish and self centered. I look back and the feeling is strong that it wasn't her I was leaving at all. I was leaving Key Largo and the routine of an 8-4 life with weekends and the summer neatly laid out, nothing changing and it was going to be like this until I retired. She was part of the whole picture and I did not separate her from the life that was putting out my fire. Could I have taken her with me and would we have been happy? It is done. Don't look back, you can never look back.

I left Jessie behind and only saw her one more time. It was that following year as I passed through Key Largo. We met by chance when I stopped at a dive shop owned by a friend of mine from those early Key years. She saw me first, came to me and said hello in that voice that took me from nowhere to 7 years with her instantly. From behind the counter came the voice of Ray, the owner, "Don't forget dinner tonight at 6 Babe". Message received. I smiled and left and didn't want to see her again. I wondered when I passed the shop on occasion how she ended up and it hurt to think about it. I never stopped in again but passing it got easier when the name changed and I didn't see Ray's car there anymore. I don't know if I should envy couples who find each other early in life and stay together, or if I am looking at lives spent in quiet desperation, making compromises in being happy until it is too late or too scary or too dangerous to leave. Each parting is a form of grieving if you cared at all. I have grieved many times.

YOU WERE ALWAYS ON MY MIND

Johnny Christopher, Mark James, Wayne Carson / Willy Nelson

By that time Grandpa had died in a nursing home and I returned for his funeral, devastated that I had not been with him. I got the call from my mother 6 months later that Pop was in the hospital and it didn't look good. I drove all night straight to the hospital and found him comatose, struggling to take a breath. Mom was tired, having been with him day and night for 2 days. I told her to go get some rest and that I would stay with him until she got back.

If you want to know about someone's medical condition, don't ask the doctor, ask a nurse. I went to the desk on the floor and talked to a nurse whose name tag said she was "Sue". She showed me the "Do not resuscitate" order Mom had signed. I asked her how long she thought Pop had and she looked me straight in the eyeballs and said, "I would give him 24 hours, maybe." She went on to explain that he had had a series of heart attacks beginning years ago, probably because his damaged lungs couldn't get him enough oxygen. Once he had the first one he was even more compromised and he started crashing in a downward spiral of lungs and heart that could only end one way. I went back into his room and took his hand.

"Pop, I am here." No response.

This tough old German never showed me how he hurt. He never asked for anything. He was always there for me and I could not remember us ever touching each other and I just wanted to touch him. The monitor over his bed showed what was left of his heart beating about 140 beats a minute. His chest, shaped like a chicken breast from sucking for air, rose and fell without regularity. I knew Sue was right. I left the room to grab a sandwich. I hadn't eaten since the night before. When I returned a half hour later Sue met me smiling.

"Someone wants to talk to you."

I walked into his room and the old man looked at me.

"This is rough." he said. About as much emotion as he could display.

For the next 5 minutes we talked as though we were young again and sitting around the campfire until he said, "I am tired and I want to sleep."

"O.K. Pop." He turned his head away and went back into the coma. I sat back trying to comprehend what had just happened. From the doorway Sue said, "Sometimes they give the people they love a gift."

Mom came back a short time later and I told her what had happened. She sat with him for a few more hours and switched off with me again. She walked out, I sat down next to him, took his hand, said "Pop, I am here". The monitor went flat. Did he wait for me to be there or did he wait for her to leave? I will always wonder.

About six months later Mom called me to tell me she had been invited to go to Cape Cod for a vacation with a guy who knew both she and my father in high school. Guess he couldn't wait any longer than that after Pop's death. I wished her well. When she began to tell me he had separate bedrooms, of course I couldn't take it anymore. I only wanted her happy. She married him less than a year after the first date and she moved to Cape Cod.

I left for Key West, the repository at mile marker 0 for expatriates, adventurers, opportunists, writers, artists, losers, lost souls and those with alternative life styles who provided the local character for tourists thinking they would see Ernest Hemingway in every bar. Hemingway was there from 1928-1939 when he wasn't in Cuba. He was there with Tennessee Williams, who outlasted him until 1983. Jimmy Buffett tuned into the culture and perfected his personification of the life style playing the bars on Duval Street. Between Hemingway and Buffett the snare was set for any normal person who wanted to say he had experienced the Key West Life Style to bar hop into oblivion. For the locals this is a love-hate relationship. We love your money. Good, leave it here, now go home. Every year it's popularity chips away more and more of the local flavor the tourists come here to experience. In the 70's and 80's it was much more authentic. Today cruise ships disgorge thousands for a few hours and the harbor area has become tee shirt shops and stores with the same shit they can buy on the ship itself or at anyone of the 3 other ports they will stop at for a few hours. The real Key West is being condensed into areas further and further south, up and off Duval. This is a balancing act.

April 23, 1982 was a major event in the legend that is Key West. K.W. seceded from the United States and became "The Conch Republic." The U.S. Border Patrol set up a road block to ensnare illegal immigrants making their way from Cuba and to try to make a dent in the drug trade. The road block was actually at the other end of the Keys, right by The Last

Chance Saloon where you begin the drive into Key Largo from the mainland. But Key West, being the spiritual leader of the Keys, declared itself a "Republic", named a Prime Minister, declared war on the U.S., immediately surrendered, and applied for a billion dollars in war reparation. See Peter Seller's 1959 movie "The Mouse That Roared". The Prime Minister kept alive the long tradition of Key Wester's wicked sense of humor and ability to exploit opportunity for personal gain. The road block slowed down the flow of tourists and supplies and that hit us in the wallet. It did stem the flow of tractor trailers leaving the Keys with enough pot to supply the nation. The Conch Republic flag earned it's place in history alongside "Mile Marker 0" signs and "Southernmost", a term used to describe every hotel, boarding house and bar seeking Key West character.

Key West can thank it's existence to Henry Flagler, the former partner of Rockefeller in Standard Oil. Flagler was largely responsible for creating the tourist industry in Florida. His hotels reached down the east coast from St. Augustine to Miami. He built the railroad that connected them to the upper states. The rich and famous came there to party. Flagler saw further opportunity. France had started the Panama Canal in 1881 but stopped the project because of the mortality rate on the workers. The U.S. took it over and completed it between 1904 and 1913. At one time Key West was the wealthiest city in Florida because of the salt industry, fishing and turtle hunting, cigar making and ship salvage. The products bound for the mainland were carried on shallow draft sailboats and it was slow going. The City had fallen on hard times by the time Flagler figured, that when the Canal was completed, Key West would be the closest U.S. port and he could increase his fortune. The railroad was labeled by some "Flagler's Folly", an engineering task that was impossible. Flagler opened his overseas railroad to Key West in 1912 and it operated until 1935 when sections were wiped out by a hurricane. The whole length was converted into the road I traveled. Flagler's monumental concrete supports held it up all the way into the 1980's until new bridges were constructed. The great government social engineering experiment called Prohibition came in 1920. It made criminals out of people who never would have broken the law otherwise. It drove drinking underground in plain sight, created an illegal industry of vast proportions controlled by the Mob and gangsters and smugglers, and many rich families who profited from it. Flagler's railroad had created the Keys, and Key West was in the shipping business.

The drug of choice for my generation kind of morphed from alcohol to pot and a combination of the two. When my band was playing the weed was going between sets and we drank Southern Comfort and gargled with a mouth wash that deadened our throats. Originally pot was pretty benign. It wasn't laced with crap and you paid for it based on it's natural quality. During college we were pretty naive. One of my roommates listened to Donovan's song "Mellow Yellow" and actually tried smoking dried banana peals. By the time I got to the Keys the pot was arriving in vast quantities and literally leaving in tractor trailers. Fishing guides made runs along the mangroves and pulled in "square grouper", bales of weed that had washed up during the night. It wasn't nasty, the locals made a few bucks, or a lot of bucks, depending on their involvement. The Key's became even more mellow than they had been solely on alcohol. So when is the government going to figure out that when there is demand for a product, making it illegal creates criminals out of people who just want to go about their personal lives?

When I decided to leave Key Largo and teaching, I had a skill set that made finding work in the Keys easy. Floyd was a local captain for whom I had been running a weekend dive boat in Islamorada. He was a good guy and he liked me and Jessie. He and his wife Kate didn't understand why I was leaving her any better than I did. He gladly gave me a job running a 6 pack dive boat out of Key West. I had a tonnage license to run bigger boats, but I liked the personal contact and satisfaction coming from running a boat for six people who I could give a personal experience to. I had plenty of money, so I rented an apartment just off Duval on Julia Street.

My bar of choice was The Green Parrot just across the street from the entrance to the Truman Annex Naval installation. The sailors and locals kept the vibe going and it was just off the tourist path. I settled into the island style of being on the water with the tourists all day and sitting on the same bar chair every night. I rarely went to the tourist joints on Duval where everyone was trying to out-Hemingway Hemingway. If I really hit it off with one of my guided dives and they wanted to meet me there I might. When I got bored with that I would break it up by going to the Pirate's Den, a strip joint in a courtyard down by Mallory Square. I got to know the "Wenches" really well. They knew that I wasn't going to pay them for a lap dance but I always watched to get the pump primed if the tourists weren't tipping. They would kind of look over at me and I would get up and move to the stage where they would kneel down and whisper in my ear while I put a $10 bill in their garter. There was no other place to put it. I was a safe haven for them if they wanted to take a break from hustling or if a jerk they were trying to fleece became too aggressive. They knew I was good to them and they were nice to me, nothing more. Honest relationship.

Floyd had plans. When he asked me to come over for dinner with him and Kate I knew he had something in mind. He was a very successful business man, in his forties with a keen interest in boats. He and Kate sailed a 26 foot sailboat down from Virginia right after they graduated college. They chose Islamorada to launch a one boat, back country fishing charter. They ran it out of what had been the fishing club for Zane Gray and his fishing buddies, now home to a small fleet of back country fishing guides. Kate took a job behind the bar at the Lorelei just down the road. They were nice people, smart and hard working. They lived on the 26 footer until they could afford a trailer in the park next to where Kate worked. It didn't take long before Floyd had a full calendar, booked in advance by referrals. One boat became two. Then he added a dive boat that sailed out of Marathon. He hired the crews and ran between the operations and Kate held down the office and they grew the shit out of it.

Floyd had a talent for hiring good people and Kate had a talent for organization. They set their sights on Key West and I came into the picture. Their home was one of the old "conch" houses that are treasured in Key West. You can find 'em but you might not be able to afford one. Many have become bed and breakfast places for those who want to vacation Key West style. They are the true character of the island and this one was typical. It was separated from the sidewalk by a low white wall with a banyan tree that barely fit in the front yard and shaded almost the whole house and lot. The walls were bright white and there was a natural wood balcony running the width of the house. The roof was gray/blue metal, pitched sharply to run off the every day at 3pm summer showers. Big slatted hurricane shutters in color to match the roof were hinged at the top and propped open at the ready. The design of these homes fit the climate in the days before air conditioning. If a hurricane hit, they were your protection because storm prediction was imprecise and you probably couldn't make it to the mainland anyway. The home had been built before 1900 by a ship's captain. It had seen it's share of successful families making their living off the sea. Kate put out a fine dinner and fit in enough questions about how things were going for me to know that I wasn't here to just enjoy her cooking.

After she pre-screened me, Floyd led me across the hundred year old wide cypress planked floors to his man cave. The room was 10xl0 at the top of the outside back steps. 50 years ago this was where seamen stripped down and left foul weather gear and the clothes and boots worn at sea before stepping into the civilization the house offered. He had left the walls the exposed inside of the planking and the frame timbers that held it together. The only real change he made was to replace the single, tiny rear window next to the door with a picture window that overlooked a small patio with a hot tub. Kate must have given Floyd the o.k. sign because she left us to a good bourbon and great Cuban cigars.

"So, we're glad to have you on board." He paused to light his cigar and to give me time to answer.

I kept it general, "Glad I am here."

Thrust and parry, no points scored by either side.

"You planning to stick around?" Floyd knew the Keys bred drunks and burn-outs or transformed expatriates into new locals who loved the life and were as good to it as it was to them.

I paused to fire up my Cuban. "I can't picture myself anywhere else."

Time to double down. "I appreciate being asked to hang out with you, but I don't think I am here just to eat Kate's food and smoke your cigars." I was careful to work Kate into the response.

Floyd settled back, satisfied I was on board, and laid out for me what he had in mind.

He had bought a small marina on Stock Island, the .9 square mile piece of ground that was the gateway to Key West, separated from it by the low, short bridge, really just an extension of the highway. Stock Island was mostly residential, aside from the golf course which was on the bay side of

U.S. I. The marina was on the ocean side, sandwiched next to the naval air installations as everything on Stock Island was. Surrounding it was cheap residences where many of the locals working jobs in Key West shacked up. In the mornings the parade of characters on bicycles and motor scooters stretched into the city.

Floyd wanted me to listen and I didn't interrupt. He had plans to begin a boat building operation, not big stuff, flats boats up to 19 feet for the bay fisherman. These boats were platforms for fisherman casting by sight to bonefish, permit and a host of other species, the fish that had brought serious fishermen here for generations. He explained that he had taken one of the boats he was about to retire and used it to "splash" a new hull. He told me about turning it upside down and altering it for his ideas of how the hull would run better and be more stable at rest for casting. He built up the sides another 6" to raise the deck from which to cast. That gave the fisherman more visibility. The old hull became the "plug" over which was laid fiberglass that hardened into a mold. The plug was discarded and the female mold was ready to pop out boat hulls. No different than using a mold to lay in a pie crust. A mold was also made for the deck that would be popped out and bonded to the hull. The secret to the quality of the new boats would be how fair the mold was made. The finished boat hull was high gloss and would show every imperfection in the mold. Floyd had hired the best fiberglass mechanic he could find in the Keys and I had no doubt his standards for finishing the boat would be just as high.

What he wanted from me was to run the boat building operation. I had fooled around building a few wood boats when I was a kid, but fiberglass construction was still developing in the early 80's and I knew shit about it. Floyd knew that too. He didn't need me to build 'em, he needed me to ramrod the deal and integrate production with sales and marketing. A large part of it would be to take customers for demo rides and to make the rounds of the boat shows with the product. He and Kate recognized more about me than I might have known about myself.

He didn't have to twist my arm. The life of a charter captain didn't vary. It was all day, every day on the water with a new group of tourists. I was o.k. with the money but I was getting restless to get on with what I had moved here for. I wanted to own my own business and I could have gone that way but here was Floyd handing it to me. I trusted him and he trusted me. More importantly, so did Kate.

I settled into a shanty office next to the metal military surplus open building that was pumping out boats. It took about 10 minutes for me to figure out that Pedro had the production end wired and that all I needed to do was leave him alone. I got into the sales and marketing right away. A couple of local guides had deposits on the first couple of boats, but we needed branding to take this product beyond the Keys.

Working trade shows is an art form if done right and a nightmare if you don't know what you are doing or don't enjoy it. I piloted and fished hull #1 in all kinds of weather. I really shook the product out on demo rides for clients, most of whom initially were charter captains who knew me and weren't afraid to tell me what changes they wanted made. Check, I knew what I was doing. I had always enjoyed client contact and was patient with fisherman. I wrote, starred in, narrated and produced a 9 minute VCR tape of the boat in action and me enjoying the hell out of it. Check, I was a people person. I got myself organized with a Suburban towing the demo boat, the signage for the booth, the brochures and the VCR and set out for boat shows.

BOATS TO BUILD

Jimmy Buffett

I began doing the weekend boat shows in Florida. Most were small, 2 day affairs over weekends. I would set up my 10x10 canopy, put the table with the brochures and 2 chairs and VCR under it and pull the boat next to it. The boat created a lot of interest in Florida and soon I expanded our presence into shows all over the south. This was not only a great boat for the flat water of the Keys, but it looked and fished like it was made for freshwater bass fishing. I put a 200 horse motor on the transom and the thing would do almost 70 miles an hour. It generated a lot of interest from "tire kickers" or just plain nice folks who couldn't afford it. When someone comes up to you at a show and starts talking the product you never know where the sale is going.

The biggest show in the country was The New York Boat Show. When I lived in Jersey I went there a lot. I hadn't seen cold weather in years and going to New York City in January was not appealing. Floyd was happy with sales and we had doubled the size of the manufacturing operation. He and I agreed to expand our presence and give it a go.

I drove straight through to north Jersey in the Suburban, towing the boat, 27 hours. West Orange was only a half hour from the Lincoln Tunnel and I vowed to swing through the old neighborhood on the way back. I arranged a hotel on the Jersey side on Route 3 about 5 minutes from the Tunnel. It cost 1/3 the price in New York and was much quieter. Doesn't matter what time of the day or night it is, New York is non-stop noise and I wasn't used to that anymore. You don't carry anything into the show. The unions do that. You don't park where you are not supposed to or you can retrieve your car at the impound yard down by the Hudson River. You don't leave from Jersey for NYC after 7am for a 9am show or you will never get there given the commuter traffic. Hurry everywhere. It took me about 5 minutes to remember why I loved the Keys.

The only break you get from talking to people for 10 straight hours is when you go to the food area and lounge reserved for the show participants. I stood in front of that 9 minute VCR loop for 5 straight days. For 5 straight days, every 9 minutes I heard myself say "The best 19 foot fishing boat the sport has to offer is right here, right now!--------------------------". My subconscious kept repeating it over and over and over. Every 9 minutes, for 5 days.

You get to know the show participants and I ran into an old friend, The Commodore. He revealed to me that his name was Bert, but professionally he was always The Commodore. I am sure it was a shock to show goers to see a midget sitting on the flybridge of a miniature trawler. I guess that today the term "midget" is socially incorrect, however it didn't bother The Commodore. In fact he loved the advantage it gave him and he played it up. His whole schtick was based around his size.

THE COMMODORE'S BOAT CLEANING PRODUCTS

½ THE EFFORT - ½ THE TIME

ASK ME HOW TO MAKE BOAT CLEANING A SMALL JOB

The sign in gold letters covered the back partition of his booth. Everything he had was white trimmed in gold. This included the labels on the fiberglass cleaner, upholstery cleaner, vinyl cleaner, chrome and brass cleaner and windshield cleaner he was hawking. He wore a starched white uniform with the gold epaulettes on his shoulders and "Commodore" embroidered on his shirt and across his gold brimmed hat. In front of the booth, and just low enough to not cover the sign, was the replica boat used for his demo's. He had commissioned this beauty to be custom built. It was just 10 feet long and an exact replica of a 40' trawler right down to the brass fittings, propellers and tinted windows. When he sat on the flybridge he was eye to eye with a six foot customer and that made it easy for him to work a show in comfort. I enjoyed the Commodore's company. When we took a break we usually took it together. He was one of the funniest and most sociable people I have ever run into. His banter with customers never stopped and it was not unusual for a small crowd to be gathered around his booth while everyone else working the show was looking at the paint on the ceiling. He didn't have to be doing this. He owned the company, not just the distribution end, but the manufacturing as well. One smart guy.

An integral part of his schtick was a female model wearing white short-shorts, a white tailored blouse cut low down the front and a sailor's round hat perched on her head. High heels were a necessity and his requirement was that they had to be gold. There was always competition to get the best looking models to draw attention to the products. The Commodore always picked them up from the local modeling agencies. He had been doing this long enough so that the agencies knew he paid over scale and that the models enjoyed working with him. The model's job was simple: Apply fiberglass cleaner to one spot on the hull, stand just so and bend slightly at the waist so that the view was great whether the customers approached form the bow or the stern. That spot on the hull had been polished so many times it wouldn't have mattered if she used the product or not. The light shining on it was blinding compared to the reflection off the rest of the hull.

Now the boat itself, in addition to being a great eye catcher, was very utilitarian and this is where the Commodore's intelligence and ingenuity really shown. As you know, the flybridge allowed him to sit down and be eye to eye with the customer while not obscuring the model whose outfit greatly resembled Betty Boop. It also housed all his back-up printed material and the bottles of product. His sales were always brisk and he had the union guys carry in boxes and place them in the boat every morning. He also had a 6 foot berth running the length of the starboard side so that he could take a nap if he wanted to while on the road. Most shows he and I shared a bourbon at the end of the day. Damn that man could drink, and I could count on a him to have a couple of fifths of Wild Turkey and glasses where the galley would have been in a full size boat. The windows were tinted so that you couldn't really see in when he had the little back door closed. I relied on him for the bourbon and he relied on me for Cuban cigars.

After 5 days the show was wrapping up the following day and we had all about had it. My mouth was permanently frozen in a smile, my voice was getting hoarse and 5 days of listening to myself saying, "The best 19 foot fishing boat the industry has to offer is right here right now------------", would leave me intellectually impaired even though I did my best with Wild Turkey and cigars at the close of each show to erase it from my mind.

The agencies took good care of him when it came to getting models, but this time he had hit the jackpot. "Dawn", sure, they were all either that or "Skye" or "Blaze", Dawn was most likely just out of high school. She was really sweet and was serious about doing the best she could for The Commodore. He treated her well and gave her an extra $20 at the end of every day. What she was doing wasn't brain surgery: Wax on wax off while bending slightly at the waist and standing just so. But she put more into it than any model he had before and he saw she was not stupid and he tried to teach her everything he could about handling the customers. As the days went on she became really good at this and The Commodore and I agreed that she had a future in customer service. It took him the 5 full days to convince her she should stay for a while when the show closed and have a drink with us. She was always running at closing time. This was the last night and the last chance. I didn't know if she was even of age, but that didn't stop The Commodore from persisting. When the last customers had left the floor I went over to his booth and sure enough, there was Dawn standing by the back door of the trawler with a coke cup in her hand. The Commodore had his and within seconds he poured me mine. We didn't want to offend her so neither one of us fired up a cigar. You weren't supposed to smoke on the floor, but after 5 days the union guys knew us. We tipped them and they loved my Cubans. I drank with them for about a half hour and it became obvious Dawn was feeling the juice. We had her laughing and enjoying herself and The Commodore was beyond charming. I was tired, getting a little high and called it a night. I left them laughing and having a great old time.

The next morning I arrived back at the convention floor to a great commotion. The floor was over 40,000 square feet, but I had no trouble hearing a guy yelling and screaming and it was coming from way over where the boat product displays were. I couldn't make out what he was yelling about until I got close enough to see it was coming from The Commodore's. This guy was BIG and LOUD and it was a good thing it was before show hours because no one was doing anything but watching. Even the Union guys were standing around and you really didn't want to mess with Union New York.

"Elvira, get the hell out of there!" Who the hell is Elvira??????????

Just then Dawn's head appeared through the open side window of the replica boat's salon. First time I had seen her without her Betty Boop hat. She was yelling at "Clifford" to shut up and how he was ruining her career and she hadn't done anything other than have a drink and she fell asleep and the show was starting in a half hour. The Commodore was nowhere that I could see. The big guy was yelling at her to get out and she was yelling at him to shut up and the few of us who were there were beginning to get into the show. He's pulling on the back door of the boat and it won't open and she is yelling at him that she can't get out that way and that she is coming out the window. First she throws out the high heels, then she throws out the hat, then she sticks her head out and puts her shoulders through. That is about as far as she got due to the fact that the modeling agency had provided The Commodore with one of the better built young ladies. There was no way those puppies were going to fit through that window without some assistance. So she starts yelling at big loud dude to grab her under her arm pits and pull while she used her hands to cup herself and flatten them out as much as she could. When she got the top end out she was only half way there and those absolutely stunning hips and buns were a challenge too, but he had her in an around-the-waist lock and she popped out. Her feet never hit the floor as he swung her around in some type of what looked like a dance move where the guy swings the girl around his shoulders. He carried her like a sack over his shoulder with that gorgeous butt and legs in our direction. Her voice eventually trailed off as they disappeared from the trade show floor but not before we heard her say, "This is my life and just because you are my brother you don't have any right to ruin it." I found The Commodore passed out on the berth where he spent the day sleeping it off. And that is how the legend of "The Midget and the Model Of The Boat Show" was born.

ELVIRA

Dallas Frazier/The Oak Ridge Boys

The following morning I turned the Suburban West on Route 3, away from NYC. The show had been successful. I had made only one direct customer sale, but the interest on the part of dealers and marinas that catered to fresh water fisherman in the Northeast was high and I added to our growing list of retailers who wanted to carry the product. I left with the belief we had a winner and that we should add more sizes to our line up.

The most direct route to ride past my old neighborhood would have been to take the Garden State Parkway south and drive 10 minutes to exit 145 in East Orange. That would have put me one block from South Orange Avenue and a few blocks from Grandpa's store and the site of the Newark riots. I wasn't going home to get angry. I was going home to feel the warmth and nostalgia of good times and so I kept going west on Route 3 until it became Route 46. I got off at Passaic Avenue and drove past Caldwell Airport where Aunt Ruth had assembled bomb sights. I worked my way through Verona and into West Orange and down Pleasant Valley Way and I wondered exactly where Carol King lived when she wrote about it. I drove up the back side of the first mountain and I discovered the golf driving range had been replaced by a shopping center.

The turn that took me past St. Cloud Presbyterian Church brought the flood of emotion I was looking for. The name of the Pastor on the sign had changed and I gave up hope of seeing Pastor Mills but the good memories flooded back. Further down I passed the house where Ginny Duenkel, the Tokyo Olympic gold and bronze medalist lived and remembered when her mom drove us to swimming practice. Down and to the right I passed the driveway where I half expected to see Karl's maroon Chevy. I turned onto the flat part of my old street and I had remembered it as much longer. The hill at the end of the school path didn't look as steep. I paused in front of my house. There was a swing set on the side and that made me happy to think my room had another child. I looked across to see if Father James was pressed against the window watching us play kicking goals. For just a flash my minds eye did see him and then he was gone. So was I. The child becomes the man and at some point the man wants to become the child again.

GLORY DAYS
Bruce Springsteen

The day after I returned Floyd and I spent almost all day covering the changes we wanted to make to take production to the next stage and he charged me with putting the dealer network in place. Then we moved the business meeting to the Green Parrot. I sensed that he wanted to talk about something other than business. I was ready. It had been an intense week, a day driving to the show, 6 days on my feet for 10 hours a day making nice-nice and a day driving back. The long neck Buds hit me quickly.

We made small talk until he got to the point.

"You ever dream about doing something and want it so bad you can't put it off anymore?" "Of course I have, that's what brought me to the Keys to begin with", I responded.

"Nah, I am not talking generalities here. Haven't you ever wanted to do something that really turns you on and gets you going, something outside of the work, the home, all the daily bullshit?"

"You mean you brought me here to tell me you want to fuck up what appears to me to be your perfect life? Why don't you try to have a kid?"

Floyd laughed but got serious.
"I am a lucky man." He avoided the kid issue.

"I have reached a point where, thanks to you running the boat building and my office manager and Kate handling the charter boats, I can back out of the day-to-day. Had years of it. We started down this road because we love the water. But it's become too much like work for me."

"Why don't you spend more time on that sweet Formula you bought?" I asked.

"Exactly!", Floyd said. Where the hell was this going?

Then he laid it all out. He had bought a 30 foot Formula for he and Kate to use personally. This was a performance boat. With two Chevy big blocks, even though they were mild and designed for pleasure use, it would do 80mph. That was much faster than most people wanted to go on the water. He had ordered the hull a bright white and set it off with two hot pink and sea foam green stripes that followed the curve of the deck line from bow to stern. The cockpit had two heavily padded bolster seats forward and a seat the width of the boat aft all plush padded white vinyl with sea foam green trim. The engine hatches were hidden under the upholstery matching 6x8 foot sun bathing deck all the way in the back where Kate spent a lot of time. Down below the forward deck the cabin had just enough room for the two of them to spend a night on board if they wanted. He kept it at the marina under cover and put it in when he wanted to use it. Treated it like a baby. I loved the Formula boat brand. They were made in Florida and top quality. Would Floyd have bought anything that wasn't?

He switched it up and steered us into a discussion of offshore powerboat racing and how he had watched racing for years in Key West. He wouldn't be content until he tried it himself. Kate wasn't big on the idea. But she was thankful for the life they had made and respected Floyd and loved him and knew it was smart to let him play.

I sucked down the long neck and ordered a shot of rum. It was going to be a long talk.

Give a boy anything with wheels or a propeller and you can bet he will want to see how fast it can go. Give a man anything with wheels or a propeller and you can bet he will want to race against other men. Give guys who see the potential to make money an opportunity and they will organize races. Give races to the public, and if they like what they see, you have created a sport.

When you mention offshore racing boats to anyone vaguely familiar with performance boats the first question is, "You mean Cigarette boats?" Well yes. Don Aronow, a retired builder from New Jersey, moved to Miami in the 1960's and began building fast boats. How do you market fast boats? You race them. He, probably more than any other person, was responsible for increasing the popularity of performance boats. Among his clients were George Bush and Lyndon Johnson. His many brands included the iconic

Cigarette, but he also developed and marketed Formula, Magnum, Donzi, and Cary.

Gar Wood, legendary designer and racer had set the stage. In 1916 he raced "Miss Detroit" to a world speed record of 74.870 mph. By 1932 he had it up to 124.860 mph but these were flat water records set in boats that could never have ventured into rougher water. That type of racer evolved into Hydroplane racing which uses lakes and rivers. That is not to say Gar didn't design and race in rougher water. The things these guys had in common was the intelligence and scientific mind to innovate and then the guts to get in what they created and risk their life doing what no one had done before. It also took a lot of cash.

New York saw the need to form a governing body. The American Power Boat Association was created in 1903. The Union Internationale Motonautique, UIM, is the world governing body. There are many types of power boats racing. Kids can kneel in a shingle with an outboard motor and race around buoys in calm waters, or you can launch a 50 foot "Superboat" off ocean rollers.

Key West is perhaps the greatest venue in the world to watch offshore power boat racing. The races start and end in the harbor right at the end of Duval Street. Over the years the course outside the harbor has changed, but efforts have always been made to bring the boats along Mallory Square as close as possible to thousands of spectators. When a boat with a 1000 horsepower or more passes a hundred feet away at full throttle it is an organ shaking visceral experience. When a group of them come in together, all jockeying for position to make the turn at the end of the harbor, no place in the world can equal the spectator experience.

Key West also provides the perfect atmosphere. Outlaws and pirates stoke testosterone fueled vicarious adventures. "Cigarette" was a legendary pirate boat that prayed on rum runners during prohibition. The pirate image was not lost on Aranow and the pirate image has never been lost on Key West. NASCAR grew out of moon shining liquor and cars fast enough to outrun the law driven by drivers who had to be fearless to be successful. Thank Prohibition and then illegal marijuana, for the development of fast offshore boats and the crews that knew how to run them. Every racer knows the fans love the exotic. Fans also love the outlaws. Just ask Willy Nelson or the late Waylon Jennings.

Floyd and Kate had been involved on the edges as long as the races had been in Key West. They took spectators on their charter boats and lined the course outside the harbor, usually right at the turn coming back in. That way the fans could see the boats in rougher water. Racing was a money maker for them and for the whole city. Floyd knew there was a whole national and regional circuit under APBA but he had never seen a race outside of Key West. The Formula had given Floyd the bug and Kate was not entirely happy and not all in. She had reason.

In November the best racers in the sport come to Key West. In 1985 Mike Poppa and Dick Fullam died just outside Key West Harbor when they lost control of "Still Crazy", a 38' race boat in rough conditions. They were trapped with the wreckage in 35 feet of water but the injuries showed they were most likely dead on impact anyway. Kate hadn't seen the accident but she sure knew about it. Ten more had died in their boats racing offshore between 1972 and 1985.

Floyd was no fool and he certainly didn't have a death wish. He had the money to do it right and Kate reluctantly agreed on the condition that he made it as safe as possible. In the Spring of 1985 Floyd steered the Formula out of Key West for the short run to Marathon. Marathon was the first race of the year and the three of us were going there to do our homework and learn as much as we could. Floyd's plan was to acquire the hull he wanted and to have me and Pedro build it up in the yard. He already had the engine builder he wanted. We tied up at Key Colony Beach 2 days before the race and proceeded to do our homework. There were many types of boats and several divisions. Class was in session.

Until 1960 offshore power boats were essentially modified pleasure boats. Same deal as NASCAR with stock bodied Fords, Chryslers and Chevys off the dealer's floors. Races from Miami to the Nassau in the Bahamas and back, 184 miles was typical. In 1956 the average speed of the winner was 19.7 miles an hour and had more to do with boat and crew absorbing punishment than how fast the boat could go. This resulted in a lot of busted boats and a lot of busted men. Ray Hunt is credited with coming up with the concept of the "deep vee" hull. Until then boat bottoms meant to handle rough conditions went from pointy at the front or bow, to flat at the back or stern. Hunt made the bottom a constant vee, bow to stern, and blew away the competition in the 1960 Miami to Nassau, Bahamas race. The new design pierced the Gulf Stream waves instead of slamming across the top. The last year of the race from Miami to the Bahamas and back was 1975 when Rocky Aoki won with an average speed of 76.6 mph in a 35 foot deep vee. APBA made it a spectator sport by bringing the races closer to the beach.

By the time Floyd dragged me in we had a lot of decisions to make based on how technical the whole thing had become. Now the deep vee hulls doing close to 100 mph in the right conditions had a challenger. Catamarans, boats with 2 hulls separated by a "tunnel" down the middle had the potential to be faster. Speeds were now over a hundred for smaller cats that could pack air between the hulls and become essentially weightless wings. They flew over the ocean suspended on top of the bottom half of their propellers. The deep vees still had the advantage in rough water, but the cats ruled when it was flat. There were 3 professional classes based on the hulls and the power and 4 "club" classes for more casual racers who didn't want to go as fast, devote the effort, or more times than not, didn't have the money to compete with the big boys. And yes, there was a woman with more chops then the men. Betty Cook was a racing legend and won more titles than most of the guys she was competing against.

Safety was at the top of the list for Kate and Floyd knew it. Technology was changing things fast. Wood had given way to fiberglass and aluminum. Builders were learning how to use cores made of balsa or matting that made hulls light and strong and engines were evolving along with hull technology. The result was racers having the potential to do over 100 mph whether the sea conditions allowed it or not. There were over a hundred boats there for us to look at spread over those 7 classes. Floyd wanted to win, but racing in a lower class was a hollow victory as far as he was concerned. We ruled out the 4 club classes right away and concentrated on the 3 pro classes. We were pros in our own minds and didn't even have a boat yet.

We started at the dry pits to see the boats out of the water. The organizers had set up in the lot next to the shopping center right on U.S. 1, strategically placed so that the businesses in the area got the spectator traffic. We walked right up to the boats and the crews servicing them. Two lanes were being added to U.S. 1 and they were not open yet. Perfect for the boats to drive south a mile to the launching area. We went down there and watched the smaller boats back down the ramp and float off their trailers. Cranes swung the big boys off their trailers and into the water and it was a well organized parade. Pit crews fired them up and they idled up the bay to the marina on bay side where they would be in the water overnight at the wet pits. There the spectators could roam the docks and look into the cockpits and see the riding crews and their equipment from a few feet away.

I wasn't shy about picking the brains of the crews and neither was Floyd. We talked to any of them that would talk to us and we learned a lot from them. After a conversation Floyd would make notes on the paper he had inside the race program he carried. That night the racers and fans partied. We sat in the condo and put some order to the information we had collected. Floyd knew more about the motors and what you could do to them in each class then I did. I had an almost photographic memory for the boat itself. The missing piece of the puzzle was to watch them run on the same course at the same time.

The course map in the program showed the start on the bay side, pro classes first followed immediately by the club classes. Essentially this was the fastest and biggest starting first on down to the smallest and slowest. The start took them under the 7 mile bridge to the ocean side and then turned left taking a straight line north just off the reef. They would race north a couple of miles until they were adjacent to the airport, then turn around and head back under the bridge into the harbor. The big boys made more laps than the smaller boats. We agreed the best place to go with the Formula was the first ocean turn outside the bridge. That way we could see them coming straight out, watch them turn left and head north and catch them on the return to the bridge as well.

Floyd drove the Formula from our condo, south, outside the reef and just outside the race course already lined with the turn boats, spectator control boats and law enforcement. We had a blast. He had the bug and Kate and I held on while he throttled up and steered. He kept it safe and the boat never left the water as I watched him wrestle with the wheel and two engine throttles. I had been rodding around in the 19 foot hulls on which I had put a 200 horse motor. That little boat would do over 70 mph if the water allowed it. I was acutely aware of the need to understand how fast you could go in what conditions during the hours I had spent giving customers demo rides. The Formula was a piece of cake compared to the smaller boats I was used to. This was a joy ride and Kate got into the excitement about the whole race thing.

We positioned the boat outside that first turn and hung out idling just enough to control the boat. The number of spectator boats out here was sparse. Most spectators had walked or rode bikes to the middle of the 7 mile bridge where the boats went right under them, or they were in boats on the bayside where the water was calmer. That morning the seas were running 3-4' outside the reef and the wind was building a little but it was a beautiful, sunny Key's day.

We heard them coming before we saw them. 30 racing engines all firing at full throttle together sounds like thunder rolling in from miles away. We saw nothing until they cleared the 7 mile bridge. First we saw the helicopters like a swarm of bees riding the top of white stalks of water thrown up by the propellers. The lead boats appeared out of the white water and got a whole lot bigger a whole lot faster. Floyd had us pointing toward the bridge idling away from the yacht anchoring the orange pillow marking the first turn. The Lavin brothers in "Jesse James" led the charge and man they were flying. I put their speed at well over a hundred and they weren't slowed the slightest by the 3-4 footers coming straight on their bow. Their cat danced over the top. A couple of other cats passed and then two deep vees giving chase. We watched them throttle back and take the 90 degree turn and then hammer it again as they straightened out for the run north. The smell of high octane fuel and exhaust floating over salt water was intoxicating and I felt my senses fully engaged just soaking it up.

We turned to face back toward the bridge in time to see the rooster tails from the second pro starters. By this time we had idled a couple hundred yards inshore of the turn boat and had a front row seat as the second group thundered up on us on our starboard side. Floyd and I saw him at the same time. A cat was coming across our bow from left to right at a 90 degree angle to the other boats, way off course. We realized he had to do a right angle turn to get behind the other boats and then make the hard left at the turn boat to make the leg north. When he made the turn onto the course and hung the right he was only a hundred yards in front of us. Whoever was throttling that boat must not have had a clue, or he was pumped up this early in the race or he simply misjudged, but he never slowed as he turned. When he hit the first wave head-on the boat lifted and pointed up, hung there for a second and then came down on it's stern which slammed the bow down and the cat went from 90mph to 0 in a few yards. We watched the two orange helmets slam forward and disappear behind the white water thrown by the crashing hull and then we saw shards of white fiberglass shoot out of the spray.

When the waterfall stopped and the boat came into view it was only 25 yards away and facing back from where it had come. It was already sunk to what was left of the deck when it reappeared. We were watching one guy sliding over the side of the sinking boat. One hand tore at the chin strap of his helmet and the other was undoing his life jacket. The blood from his face was already staining his white uniform. The other guy was slumped forward in the seat and we could only see the side of his orange helmet resting against the dash board.

Floyd and I looked at each other and the totality of the situation hit us at the same time: Sinking boat, one guy with head injury about to drown and another guy who might be dead and looked like he was going to sink with the boat. Where was any kind of a race support boat? Nowhere we could see. We were it. We became aware of a helicopter appearing and hovering over the scene. The sign on the side read "Needle Nose Race Photography". Great, the drowning of the two and the sinking of the boat was going to be filmed. They were in the right place at the right time to get some great shots and we were the only help in sight.

Kate already had the anchor line out and was cutting the anchor free from it. This lady had been around boats all her life and she got it right away too. Our Formula was drifting closer to the sinking wreck and I was the strongest swimmer. I dumped my flip flops and pealed off my shirt as Kate was tying the line around my waist. Floyd was at the controls, kept the Formula broadside and his eyes never left the two orange helmets. I covered the distance in what felt like a couple of seconds keeping my head up and my eyes on the big guy who by now had succeeded in getting his life jacket off and was sliding into the water. I watched him disappear under, pulled down by his driver's suit and shoes. I got to him before he was deeper than arms length and I pulled him up by the collar of his uniform shirt. I had made plenty of pulls lifeguarding, but this guy was big and all dead weight. Kate already had tension on the line and I put him in a cross chest carry and laid him across my body. Floyd left the controls and the harder the two of them pulled the easier it was for me to keep us both up. When I got him to the swim platform at the stern of the boat he was dead weight but he was breathing and beginning to thrash around again. Floyd's eyes were still on the second guy who hadn't moved and I read them and started back to the sinking boat. I covered the water in between us the second time and pulled myself over the side of the boat which was water level. As I grabbed this guy by the collar on the life jacket he turned his head and looked me in the eyes. They were looking at me strange, but I didn't see blood and he appeared to be unmarked. There was no time to ask him where he hurt and if he had broken something and I knew I could hurt him if I moved him but there was no choice. I didn't know if he would come out from between the seat and crushed dashboard but he was able to help and together we pulled out. He let out a scream as he popped up and the boat sunk out from under us. His life jacket made the job of keeping him up easier than the first guy. That was a good thing because Kate and Floyd saw I had him and didn't stop lifting guy number one from the swim platform onto the engine hatch lounge. The guy I had was woozy, but he was able to hold the line Kate had tied to a cleat while I pulled us in.

During the whole thing I don't remember a single word being passed between the three of us. You never know who has the right stuff until you get into a jam. We now had both of them on the engine hatch lounge flat on their backs. Kate sat at the big guys head and held his helmet as straight as she could. His white drivers suit was stained red, I guessed from his nose. I knew the second guy was the throttles because that's the seat I took him from. By now he was speaking and asking what happened. I tried to tell him while Floyd was back at the controls already heading for the bridge only 2 miles away. Floyd was on the radio and being told to keep his course and a patrol boat was on the way. The Florida Marine Patrol showed up in a 24 foot center console, lights blazing. O.K., now you're in charge. Tell us what you want us to do.

They quickly assessed we had a capable boat and crew and that it was better to not move the driver and throttle man until we got to real medical help which was shore based and only a few miles in. They switched Floyd to another radio channel so they could keep in constant contact. We followed them and they kept us clear of the race course but heading directly to the medical people on shore. Floyd turned us into the berth they directed us to at the wet pits. A lot of white shirts with patches all over them grabbed the Formula and tied us up. EMT's and Paramedics swarmed the boat. The driver and throttles left on backboards with their helmets still on and restrained.

Things calmed down and Kate looked at Floyd, "So, do you really want to ask me again if I am o.k. with you doing this stuff?"

I couldn't help it. I started laughing and then Floyd started laughing and Kate wasn't laughing but we all had a group huggy and bonded over what had just happened. A guy showed up with a white official's shirt on and a big pass around his neck and handed us gold colored passes and asked us to go to the drivers awards ceremony as their guests. We stayed tied up at the wet pits until the race was over and the boats returned. We surveyed the walking wounded, destroyed equipment, happy crews, pissed off crews and all the emotions you can wring out of something like this. Floyd and I loved it.

The awards ceremony was the best thing that could have happened to get Kate on board. We walked into the room full of drivers, owners, pit crews boat and engine manufacturers, local dignitaries the volunteers who helped out and various assorted people who wanted a piece of the action. The riding crews and pit crews were easy to spot and we put names to faces and faces to the boats. We no more than stepped in and were greeted by the guy who gave us the passes. He introduced himself as Richard and we saw the APBA patch on his white shirt. He got our names and the name of our boat, asked us what we wanted to drink and sent another guy to the bar. "Come on over here, there's people I want you to meet."

We headed for a table with a guy in a flight suit and a group of women and men with shirts or complete uniforms that identified them as EMT's or paramedics. Richard introduced us as the crew of "Star Gazer", the boat that pulled out the driver and throttles of "Double Trouble". The first thing we wanted to know was what happened to the guys we pulled out. The only person at the table not wearing a uniform of some type, a young looking guy wearing a Hawaiian, shirt spoke up.

"I am Dr. Morgan. I am Chief of Staff at Fisherman's Memorial Hospital."

He was eager to shake our hands.

"We admitted both of them. The driver has a bad concussion, a broken nose and orbital socket and we are watching his lungs. He inhaled a lot of salt water. We aspirated him. The second guy has a concussion also and six broken ribs. The bulky life jacket probably saved him when he hit the dash board. We understand they de-accelerated really quickly and they probably bruised some internal organs. All in all they are going to be o.k. but it's going to take a while."

By now the uniforms had gathered around us and we were the ones answering questions. We described the rescue for them. Floyd had me do most of the talking.

We learned why the whole accident came together the way it did. Offshore racing is a logistical nightmare for those organizing the race. The morning of the race an army of volunteer EMT's and nurses and doctors give physicals to all participants in the riding crews to make sure nobody racing is hung over, doped up or physically screwed up. The longer the course, the more support needed from medical, law enforcement and race volunteers. This was a long course. Two miles from the start to the bridge, 2 more to the first turn, 4 North along the reef, 4 back south then the 4 miles back to the start, 16 linear miles. A yacht and 2 large orange "pillows" set 300 yards apart mark the start and finish line. A paramedic boat stands by at the start/finish. The boats are led out of the wet pits by law enforcement and assemble in the "milling area" a half mile behind the start. The biggest and fastest pros start first and the groups work their way down to the smallest boats, 22-24 feet long with single outboards. That puts 50 to 100 boats varying from a 40 footer capable of well over 100 mph on the course to a 22 foot boat that can do 60 in the best of conditions at the same time. Even the milling area before the start was dangerous. On March 28, 1981,

Al Copeland, owner of Popeye's Fried Chicken, ran over the cockpit of Joel Halpern's catamaran in a 37 foot deep vee and killed him. It is very difficult to see where you are going when these boats aren't up and running at speed.

Each turn is marked by an orange pillow and a yacht. Paramedic boats and law enforcement and military, from the Coast Guard to local police departments, are stationed along the course for medical support and spectator control. The main straightaways are lined by volunteer boats flying flags to mark the spectator areas. In the middle of this particular offshore 4 mile straightaway was the usual dive and rescue boat manned by 2 rescue divers and two paramedics. Each turn boat had at least one paramedic. Support ambulances were in the pits and on land at various points along the course. Overflying the whole thing is "Angel One", a helicopter capable of flying as fast as the race boats and staffed with 2 rescue divers and paramedics.

Why we got involved became clear. Angel One was right behind the rest of the choppers filming the action when the first group of racers went by us. By the time the second group came by Floyd had been idling Star Gazer back toward the bridge traveling parallel to the course and away from the support boats at the first turn. The cat that wrecked was at the tail end of that second group and off course when he came by us. Pure chance put us at exactly the right place at exactly the right time for those two guys.

Racing on any level is not a game. On May 21, 2017 throttleman David Raabe lost his life at the Point Pleasant Grand Prix when his boat tangled with another on the first turn of the race. Rest quietly.

Richard went on to explain that the turn boat and the chopper taking still photos had immediately called in the accident. Both reported that there was a boat on the scene assisting the drivers and the Needle Nose chopper assumed we were a patrol boat equipped to handle the situation as they watched and photographed the action. Angel One was never called back from the lead pack because Race Control was told the situation was in hand. Well, it was. We were there. Phil Lewis, the photographer on the Needle Nose chopper stepped forward and handed us a picture of the rescue. All's well that ends well.

We started drinking and talking to this group and stayed to see the trophies awarded. Kate ended up with a bunch of women wearing assorted uniform shirts at the bar. Floyd made his way from driving crew to driving crew and made a lot of really good contacts, particularly when they found out he had a boat yard and fiberglass shop in Key West. I hung out with the guy in the flight suit who was the pilot of Angel One, a decorated Vietnam chopper pilot who was a legend on the racing circuit and a hoot and a half when he got into the Cuban cigars I always carried. He carried his bottle of Jim Beam and I carried my bottle of Jack Daniels and he led me from group to group where he would slap me on the back and introduce me as the guy who pulled out the crew that wrecked and someone would try to buy me a drink. It all got a little hazy after a while, but when we left and hailed a ride back to the condo, even Kate was beginning to loosen up and she was talking to Floyd again. The next morning we picked up the Miami Herald at the front desk and there was a picture of Star Gazer with me about half way back towing the second guy. The credit went to "Phil Lewis of Needle Nose Productions". Floyd had me drive the Formula back to Key West. I took the opportunity to fool around with the speed and steering to see how she ran in various conditions while Floyd talked to Kate on the back bench seat. By the time we got back it was decided. Floyd could drive his racebot under one condition: Kate wouldn't have anyone but me on the throttles.

WAVE RIDER

Omni

Lockheed Martin's F-16 jet was the first fighter aircraft to have a no frame, one piece heat molded acrylic bubble canopy. The canopy is 7.5 feet long, 33 inches wide and varies in thickness, but is .5 inches thick at the pilot's point of vision. They have a gold tint because of the gold film applied to the inside to dissipate radar. They vary in configuration depending on the mission the F-16 was designed for. The initial design specs called for it to withstand a hit by a four pound bird while traveling at 250 mph. Only a set percentage have the optical clarity and tolerances to make the cut and end up on a fighter jet. The others get stacked up as surplus. These have saved the life of many a race boat driver.

Motor sport has always been a tug of war between technology and the human who pilots the things. The 80's saw a quantum leap in offshore race boats. Outboard motor technology pushed bolt-on horsepower of one motor into the 300 horse range. Car based, big block, 454 cubic inch V8 General Motors engines formed the basis for power plants that could be modified to produce maximum horsepower for short bursts of speed before they blew up, or provide huge amounts of torque and be dependable for hours at a time. The iconic 350 cubic inch small block had more parts and accessories produced than any engine before or after and anyone could pick and choose how many horses versus how much reliability by building it up to their specifications. NASCAR mandated every aspect of how their engines were configured in order to provide a level playing field. Offshore did the same thing with the power plants of the various classes. The hulls were another matter. Speeds went from deep vees doing 80 mph to catamarans with proven potential to reach 125 or better in only a couple of years. Crew safety did not catch up right away and men died because of it.

The old thinking was that if an offshore boat went over the crew should be thrown clear of it. A three man riding crew was the norm, a driver, a throttleman and a navigator. They stood on a deck wedged into upholstered bolsters in front of a solid bulkhead and dashboard wearing thickly padded life jackets and helmets, their heads just above the level of the deck covering the front of the boat. The pounding was horrific. The list of celebrities who thought they were going for a joy ride and couldn't wait to get out of the boat is long. It is most likely topped by an ultimate tough guy. Heavy weight boxing champ Rocky Marciano rode one time and vowed to never get into an offshore boat again.

There are many ways a riding crew can get hurt. One of the worst accidents I have ever seen was a charity event where professional race drivers raced 8 foot model cats with 25 horse motors around a 100 yard closed course next to a Holiday Inn. One driver was thrown from the boat and the boat behind him ran the prop across his head. He lived and will bear the scars from the top of his head to his chin for life. I watched another guy waving to the crowd, while doing about 60 mph just off the beach, slam into a wave as the boat rolled to his side. He never left the boat. But the force of the water at only 60 slammed him back like a rag doll and he no longer has use of his right arm. Virtually all the fatalities until 1987 were riding crew either seated or standing up that were not restrained and had no windshield.

Offshore boats fly off waves. The object is to fly straight and level and have the bottom of the boat land on top of the next wave or several waves ahead depending on how fast you are going. If the boat plows into the back of one or goes into the hole between them the result can be a "stuff". The water comes over the top of the boat while you are still at speed. Not a good idea if your head is out and you have no windscreen capable of stopping tons of water. The result is that the boat either continues it's momentum and you come back up again or it stops abruptly and your body doesn't. Worst case scenario you get decapitated and/or crushed as your body and/or head hit the solid dash and firewall. In sudden de-acceleration your heart can also bounce off your ribs and sternum or tear loose from the arch of the aorta, or your head can snap forward and back severing your vertebra or brain stem.

Offshore boats can also "trip". This occurs when the boat lands too far forward on the wave and the force of re-entry on the back of the boat pushes the bow down. The result is usually a "stuff".

Offshore boats can "barrel roll". This occurs when the boat rolls over sideways, usually when taking a turn too hard or when the seas are coming in from the side and pick one side up and deposit it over the top of the other.

Offshore boats can "hook". This occurs when the driver has over steered and the bow swaps ends with the stem. This is usually accompanied by a barrel roll.

Catamarans can "blow over". This occurs when they are at high speed and either the force of the oncoming wind and/or sea conditions force the bow up until the boat does a backward somersault.

There are a bunch of other ways you can hurt yourself and your boat, but most happen too fast for the riding crew to know what the hell happened.

All of this is controlled by the throttleman or "throttles". The driver needs a light touch on the wheel and the ability to stay on course and miss things that pop up, but throttles trims the boat and decides how fast you can go in what conditions. This is not a young man's game. The only way to get experience is to do it. Throttles has one, two or three sticks next to his hand to control speed depending on whether the boat has one, two or three engines. On the dash board in front of him is a toggle switch to raise and lower the drive to which the propeller is attached, one for each engine. There are two more switches because most boats have "trim tabs" that stick out the back. These, up to 8 separate controls, are adjusted in concert to keep the boat running level front to back and side to side. Trimming the boat right is important when she flies. How you left the water has a lot to do with what is going to happen when you come back down. There is the usual bank of gauges you would expect to find for each engine, temperature, oil pressure etc. and a tachometer to show how fast the engine is revving. Throttles job is to constantly adjust the trim of the boat to maximize the speed for the sea conditions, while giving the driver the fastest possible ride that he can control steering.

The sea is always changing even if you are going in a straight line. Waves coming straight at the boat vary in size and shape and they are trying to push the bow up. When you turn across them they are trying to roll the boat sideways. If you are going into a turn you need to drop the angle of the propellers and change trim tabs to bite and hold the boat in the turn. If the driver is turning too sharp throttles can't let off on the speed or the boat will hook and either barrel roll or swap ends, similar to a spin out in auto racing. Throttles can help him out by putting on more speed and flattening out the turn, right up until the driver is still over steering and you got nothing left to give and you kiss your ass goodbye.

All this is accomplished while not taking your eyes off the water in front of the boat or the competitors beside you. The faster you go the further ahead you have to look. The cardinal sin is to over rev the engines by not pulling back the throttles when the props leave the water. If you have to look at the tachometer to do this it is way to late and you just blew up a racing engine. Floyd and I had a lot of decisions to make to dance this dance.

"Miami Vice" ran on TV from 1984-1990. The cop drama with Don Johnson set trends in fashion, firearms and fast boats. A basis for all the action was the life of the drug trade and the good guys chased the bad guys all over Miami on the water. The mood was set by some of the edgiest music ever written.

Phil Collins foreshadowed the atmosphere with "In The Air Tonight", a symphony of suspense, betrayal and pounding drums. The romanticized good guys, Crockett and Tubbs 38 foot Scarab, was so iconic that Floyd and Kate chose those colors for the boat we would run.

The real cops and robbers thing was a whole lot less glamorous. The world of offshore power boat racing saw it up close and personal. The days of opportunists making a few bucks by smuggling a couple of bales of pot was over. Pot was the common man's drug of choice along with alcohol and we saw how well Prohibition worked. So, run in some pot, make a few bucks and everyone is happy. The consumer wanted more. Pot was passe. When I was making music as a 19 year old in the Midwest we all knew that some of the older musicians were heroin users. Users were losers, they were burn outs. If you lived your life out of a guitar case wondering what town you were waking up in what would you do to dull it all? Consumers didn't want downers, they wanted uppers. Enter cocaine, enter drug cartels, enter opportunity.

There was a standing joke in offshore racing that it was easy to find a throttleman. They were in jail in the Bahamas. Don Johnson rode the good-guy-with-an-edge image into offshore racing. I shared a dock with him in Bay City, Michigan. Great! When the APBA guys told me that I would be on one side of a dock and Sonny Crockett on the other, I wondered why they looked at me like I was a sacrificial lamb. His large, deep vee, biggest in the race, was on one side of a six foot wide dock and my smaller cat was on the other. There was a clear separation of Johnson's unlimited assets, good looks and popularity, and my presence which the spectators ignored. He was dating Barbara Streisand at the time and they had a motor home stationed at the end of the dock which the fans had staked out. Fans and press deemed my boat as the closest place from which to see Johnson and Streisand up close. I spent 2 days trying to convince people they were standing on my race boat. My boat was not a stage set up on the other side of the dock from Don Johnson and Barbara Streisand for spectator convenience. I finally had enough. When a guy with a microphone asked me what it was like to be on the race course with this living legend I got creative. I told him that I had been at the driver physicals with him and he was a puny little runt but my opinion was that he did have great hair. Just then a woman behind us watched Johnson pull the crotch strap on his life jacket between his legs, and called out, "Oh Donny, I'll do that." He smiled at her and I turned and told her that I had seen him in the shower and that she would be disappointed. She looked stunned and shut up. I have no idea what Don Johnson's manhood looks like but that sure was effective. The guy with the microphone, who was using me as a pretext to get close to Don, just kind of disappeared.

The reality was that cocaine and pot smuggling had become brutal, murderous, and very profitable. 188th Street in Miami had become "powerboat row" where some of the fastest, baddest and most expensive performance boats were produced. Some were plush and ended up in the hands of weekend warriors who wanted to out perform the neighbors. Some were pure race boats. Some of those race boats ended up doing double duty as drug smugglers. Some were built to be drug smugglers.

When the Feds decided to seriously crack down on drug smuggling by chasing offshore boats carrying the stuff they turned to Aronow to build a chase boat. Aronow created "Blue Thunder", a government commissioned dark blue chase boat. The reality was that it couldn't catch the boats being built for the trade.

Here we were, racing with movie stars and guys with gazillions in the bank. Nice part is that we were competitive. We built a cat that could swap out motors to run in any one of the top 3 pro classes. We had the brains to run the third tier for a fraction of what the "Open Class" boats were running. I got to share the race course with the big boys for a fraction of the cost. We also shared the course with some really bad dudes.

By 1985 George Morales was under 23 federal indictments linked to drug trafficking. He forfeited property in the Bahamas and Miami, 12 racing boats, including several that were renowned retired champions, and 11 airplanes and helicopters along with a bunch of other stuff. Here was the blueprint for drug smuggling: Aircraft to bring the shit into the Bahamas and the go-fast boats to bring it into the U.S. He went down and was sentenced to 16 years in prison when an informant tipped of the Feds about a delivery of 3,000 pounds of cocaine. A gallon of gasoline weighs 6 pounds and therefore, 3000 pounds of drugs is equivalent to 500 gallons of fuel. Those boats in racing trim will burn at least 120 gallons of premium gas an hour. The run from the Bahamas takes less than an hour. Any of these big performance boats had the capacity to run large volumes to satisfy the American consumer.

Best we conclude the story of George Morales. He also happened to hold the World Record for Speed in an offshore boat, the speed record from Miami to New York, and won the APBA world title three years in a row. What emerged during his legal testimony was a picture of how drug smuggling helped fuel South American revolutions with the alleged assistance of the U.S. government. He was careful to not implicate anyone on the bad guy side. This got him a reduced 6 year sentence for his stellar cooperation and then a vacation to South America upon release. He soon died from either a car accident or slipping on a bar of soap in the shower. The facts are a little murky. OOOOOOOOPS

Ben Kramer came out of the Bronx to found "Fort Apache" on Powerboat Row. He built some of the biggest and baddest deep vees on the circuit. At some point Randy Lanier, a promising Indy race car driver, hooked up with him and the smuggling made them wealthy. Lanier got busted and so did Kramer. Kramer staged one of the epic prison escapes of all time. He was serving prison hell in Florida when a tiny 2 seat helicopter landed in the exercise yard and Kramer made a dash for it. Apparently Ben had gained a lot of weight in prison and the pilot did not compensate. The chopper rolled over. Another oops.

That is not the end of this story. Turns out Kramer was the great nephew of Meyer Lansky. Before he went to prison he had several legit business dealings with the father of performance boats Don Aronow. Aranow was assassinated, shot through the window of his car, on February 3, 1987. Kramer was indicted for the hit while in prison. I had lunch with his father during a race in Key West. Nice guy.

A legendary racing duo was Willy Falcon and Sal Magluta, two Miami High school boys born into modest homes. They amassed fortunes and rocketed to the top of fast powerboats. "Team Seahawk" boats dressed in their light blue warpaint won and won and won. Money was not a problem, until Falcon and Magluta were indictment in October 1991 for moving massive amounts of drugs.

And so it has ever been. Fans live the life style of fast boats or fast cars and fast living through their heroes and villains.

ANGELS LOVE BADMEN
Roger Murrah and Waylon Jennings/ The Highwaymen

Pedro lowered Floyd's black 32 foot cat into the water at the marina for the first time. Kate splashed tequila on her bow and said the boat should keep us safe. "It" then took life and became "she". We would find out soon enough what personality she had. Entry to the cockpit was down through the top of the canopies, one directly over each seat. The deck felt flimsy underfoot and it was. Inside, the boat was a welding work of art. A tubular roll cage with two aluminum NASCAR seats supported the canopies and surrounded us. The whole rig was bolted in. All the fiberglass deck did was keep out water. The boat could come apart and we would be sitting in our capsule under the canopies. We cut out the top of the canopies so that in the event we had a problem, either right side up or upside down, we would not have to fool around with latches or locks to get out. We strapped into the seats with the NASCAR approved belts. Our heads were under the front of the canopy. This met with Kate's approval.

I looked straight into Floyd's eyes through the canopies. Inside, the console between the seats was the only divider between us. My throttles and a pony scuba tank with an octopus regulator, one hose and mouth piece secured next to me and one next to Floyd, sat on top. Floyd put his steering wheel onto the shaft and snap locked it into place. There were two items I never raced without. The divers knife I had owned for 20 years was strapped to my left leg and a "spare air" tiny scuba tank with a mouth piece fixed directly to it rode on my right leg. If we were upside down and conscious it would have been no problem to breathe and cut belts to get the driver out if had to. I fired up the modified small block Chevy's that took up the space from the cockpit back. The good vibrations pulsed through the boat in the staccato uneven rhythm of racing motors that did not appreciate being held back and would soon be singing when we let her run. The boat had life and we let her idle for a bit while Pedro and the engine builder scrambled around inside the engine compartment checking for loose stuff or leaks. They got out, lowered the hatch and secured it with the two quick release hood pins. Pedro gave us thumbs up and he pushed us off the dock gently like he was releasing his baby into the world. He and the engine builder climbed into the Formula with Kate and started out of the marina.

I put her into gear and we jumped from zero to ten miles an hour. Her personality at low speed was what I expected. She was difficult to handle and uncomfortable to control as she surged and lurched, held back to a speed that was not to her liking. When we cleared the marina the Formula was turning right inside the reef and Pedro had her up to about 45. Through the intercom Floyd told me he was ready. He steered for the Formula now about a half mile ahead and I pushed the throttles forward. She shot forward effortlessly like a thoroughbred out of the starting gate and we were on plane at 60 before I knew what happened. The water was calm and we were eager. We closed on the Formula fast and as Kate took pictures we thundered by at 90. Floyd made a series of long sweeping turns and I got on and off the throttles to see how speed and wheel worked together. After 10 minutes of shaking her out Floyd told me to pull her back and he pointed her straight on a line inside the reef. I pushed the throttles forward and this time, didn't stop. 90-95-100-105-110-114 with the sweet sound of 2 racing engines at the top of their range singing. 114 didn't make us the fastest boat in the class. But she was built to last and we were as safe inside that cockpit as we could make it. Others were intent on shaving pounds in exchange for speed. We wanted to fight a lot of battles and live through them.

We turned for the marina, throttled up and damn if Floyd singing country western didn't float across the intercom while he steered at 100 mph. We were gonna be just fine.

THE CONVERGENCE

The first race of the year was at Marathon and for us it was all familiar and right down the road. Canopies were new for our friends on the safety crews and they took turns inspecting our cockpits in case they had to get us out. We learned a lot trying to position ourselves for the start and got ourselves boxed out and shuffled to the back. When they dropped the green flag we got washed down by the rooster tails of the boats in front of us and trailed them out of the bay, under the six mile bridge, past where we had pulled out Double Trouble the year before and to the first turn where we hung a left and started along the edge of the reef. Baby came into her own. The boats in front of us came back to us as our ability to handle rougher water started to show. I was refining the rough water throttles with every wave that rolled under us and Floyd was steering great. We were the only boat in the class with canopies and we weren't afraid to drive through shit and we were comfortable because we felt safe.

We reeled in 4 boats on that outside leg and then gave it back when we turned under the bridge into the calm waters of the bay. Second lap was the same and the third, but with each lap we gained on more of them and gave up less. It was lookin pretty good and Floyd was singing country western and then there was a loud bang and Floyd was having trouble steering. The one problem with canopies is that you can't see directly behind you and therefore we didn't know that the engine hatch pins had pulled loose and the hatch was laying on the outdrives. We stopped, I unbelted and took a look. We had two choices: Try to take off the rear hinges and dump the hatch and continue on, or throttle back and finish the last lap with the hatch laying on top of the outdrives. We had no tools to take it off. That was the last race I ever ran without a minimal tool kit. We finished last in class but the driver's parties were great and Kate loved her uniform shirt.

We ran ten races that season and were respectable by the time the Worlds rolled around in Key West that November. We had enough experience to know how far we could push in what conditions and Floyd and I worked like a team. This was our city and our water. Over 100 boats came from all over the place. The head of the European contingent was Fabio Buzzi, an Italian boat designer who set the Open class on it's ear with design innovations. 16 boats were in our class and all American. We had raced against them all.

Key West's legendary debauchery reaches it's peak during "Fantasy Fest", "Sail Fest", or offshore power boat racing. This stuff was routine for us. We got to do it anytime we wanted. There were three races spread over a week. Combined high points names the world champion and the party goes on for at least 7 days.

I stopped into the Pirates Den for a beer the night before the boat parade down Duval. The place was packed because the race boats were in town. The wenches were doing great and ignoring me because the big spenders were rolling cash and they didn't need me to prime the pump. By about one in the morning the crowd was thinning out. How much can you drink and still stand up? I had learned to pace myself a long time ago. Teal came over and bought me a drink. She asked if she could ride on the boat for the parade tomorrow. Of course she could.

The parade got organized at the shopping center on US 1 and took the back roads to the southern most end of Duval where the party started and didn't stop until the end of Duval at the harbor. Pedro was driving the Suburban towing Baby and we were hanging out waiting for things to start when 2 cars pulled up. Teal was the first one out followed by a total of 8 of the wenches.

"I didn't think you would mind if the other girls came too."

Mind, hell no, but I wondered what Floyd and Kate were going to say when they met us at the top of Duval to get on board for the parade. When we got there I was standing on my seat, sticking out of the canopy from the waist up and looking down the front deck at 8 luscious wenches wearing micro bikinis. Kate was priceless, "Gee I guess I am overdressed for the party." She looked real good in her white crew shirt and khaki shorts. I gave up my seat to Floyd and Kate stood on the other seat sticking up through the canopy and I was forced to sit on the deck with 8 strippers in micro bikinis.

We had just started down the street when the locals recognized who our hood ornaments were and began demanding either beads or boobs, a long standing tradition. What with Fantasy Fest or just an average Saturday night this was no big deal. Soon I was sitting with 8 topless strippers.

Kate said, "Excuse me, can we talk for a minute?" Floyd was leaning as far away from her as he could kind of looking at the roof of the store on his left. I came up to the canopy and she continued.

"My sister's 15 year old daughter and her friends are going to be at the corner of Duval and South Street."

Say no more. I called the wenches together for a huddle and they stopped drinking beer and jiggling for the crowd and gave me their full attention. I explained the situation and by the time we got to the corner we had 8 vestal virgins wrapped in beach towels waving to Kate's niece and her 3 girlfriends.

The parade ended 4 hours before the wenches had to go to work and they were grateful to me for letting them party on the boat and they felt obligated to spend the next 3 hours and 45 minutes showing me a good time before the club opened. God bless Key West.

When you get into the boats you had better be straight. The Key West race course is intense and three races over 7 days will beat up man and machine. Somewhere in all of this is a line that serious racers don't cross. Pre-race physicals for the riding crews are intended to weed out the fools who are high or hung over. Sometimes you can be super prepared and super careful and none of that matters.

The Key West race course has always produced thrills for spectators and challenges for competitors. The racing was evolving into more of a spectator sport and this brought the races in closer. The days of seeing boats leave a dock and then sit around for 4 hours until they came back was changing. The balance between spectator appeal and the true challenge of running at speed offshore varied from venue to venue. Key West provided a perfect setting for change. The debate as to what the course was going to look like centered on the reef. The Keys are protected by this shallow shelf that extends into the ocean from the little bit of dry land that is the Keys. The reef knocks down the waves coming in to land. Inside the reef you are buffered from the ocean swells. Outside you take whatever the ocean pushes at you. How fast boats can run depends on how rough the water is. Rarely does the boat with the most speed win if the sea is kicking at all. Bigger boats have the advantage. But when you are racing in your own class where all boats are about the same size, it comes down to the skill of the crew and how much you are willing to gamble. In the World Championship of 1986 the course was still running a long north to south leg outside the reef which made for more dangerous racing.

We waited with the other 15 boats in our class for the pace boat to come around and start us for the first lap. The harbor is narrow. At the end of a lap we would enter the harbor at 115 mph and scream by the Navy installation, then Mallory Square, then the long bar at the end of Duval Street and at the end the Galleon with it's boat docks. On the other side the narrow harbor is bordered by the anchorage for live aboard boats and transient boats and what used to be a low lying island of trees behind which the sun sets. Today "Money Island" is multimillion dollar houses.

The pace boat picked us up. We straightened out the circle we had been in and moved forward in a straight picket line like race horses holding back until the green flag dropped. I had learned to stay to the outside on the starts. In the middle you got sandwiched and I didn't need another boat taking us out at the start. We throttled up and the anchorage and island flew by on the right. Exiting the harbor we had about half of the class in front of us. Then the seas started to build as we closed on the outside of the reef. We didn't back off, a concert of a rough water boat that I learned how to fly and both of us enclosed in our safety cockpits. We pulled 3 of the 8 in front of us in the seas outside the reef. I had the drives tucked to keep the nose down when we flew and the rollers were nice and steady. On the far turn that took us back along the beach to the harbor I set the trim tabs and drives and gave Floyd the speed he needed for the way he approached the turn. We turned inside another boat like Baby was on railroad tracks. The turn into the harbor was a right hander marked by the big double masted sailing ship out of Maine anchoring the orange pillow. We knew the captain well and he had asked us to give his charter a thrill. Floyd took Baby within 50 feet of his stern and we could see the people on board go nuts.

The run along the naval pier and Mallory square past the long bar with a thousand fans less than 100 feet away is a trip. At the end of Duval Street is the abandoned circular concrete pad sticking 6 feet above the water. The aim is to get as close to that sucker as you can to carry speed into the turn at the end of the harbor. We could clearly see the three leaders 100 yards in front of us. By the second lap it was apparent we had the advantage outside, but those guys weren't rookies and they had the speed to stay in front. We finished 4th three races in a row. Another run at the World Championship would have to wait for next year.

APBA had stopped by and taken pictures of our canopy rig with the deck off Baby so that the construction was clear. The canopies bolted to the flange welded to the top of the roll cage made the whole thing a single unit. You could have lifted it and put it in any boat. A lot of other guys were experimenting with the canopies also. On November 6, 1986 at those World Championships, Mark Lavin and his cat, Jesse James, tripped, stuffed and killed him at a point outside the reef that had seen 2 fatalities the year before. That was it for Kate. Floyd never raced again.

Floyd and I had a special bond that can only be forged when one man trusts his life to another. I also had the complete trust of Kate. Our fishing boat sales were excellent. I had grown the production and sales to the point where we doubled the production capacity again and I had an assistant for the day to day stuff. Baby was a billboard and experienced throttles were hard to come by. I kept on. The boat name changed with each new driver and sponsor and so she was just "Baby" to me. We agreed Floyd and Kate would handle the business stuff needed to campaign the boat and line up sponsors. I would continue to throttle and break in new drivers. That was o.k. with me because the drivers were only going to go as fast as I wanted them to anyway. This arrangement took me into offshore's zenith during the campaigns of 1987 into 1989. There were a lot of big names with big bucks getting into the sport. Crew safety caught up with speed and the technology evolved into "Superboats". The whole thing became a circus show.

Al Copeland, who owned Popeye's Fried Chicken, showed up with two boats, one for rough water and one for calm water. He brought a tour bus and the "Chicken Chopper", his own helicopter that over flew the course. One trailer had a Ferrari garaged between the forks of a cats bow. Not to be outdone, Pedro and I welded a rail to the back of Baby's trailer and I put a 250cc motorcycle on it so I could get around when they flew me into the races.
Chuck Norris, Kurt Russel and Goldie Hawn, Burt Reynolds and Loni Anderson and a bunch of other names either hung around or competed.

NFL champion quarterback Joe Theismann retired from football in 1985. He raced heads up against us in a boat sponsored by Caesar's Casino in Atlantic City. Hell of a nice guy. Signed footballs for kids and threw them passes when he was on dry land. He never beat us.

Part of our sponsorship deal was that when the sponsor got the boat they got me. I was flown into wherever the race was being held and Baby would be waiting, my motorcycle on the trailer, attended to by the crew that drove her there. It was sweet not having to tow her around myself and I soaked it all up. I was tiring of it though. I had run over 40 races, regional, national and 3 World Championships. Floyd and Kate went on occasion to keep up the socializing and drum up new sponsors. That was getting old for them too and we were doing way too good selling boats to continue for much longer. How many parties can you go to? How many times can you do the same thing? It was all a show. I was ready for another change.

DESPERADO

Glenn Frey, Don Henley / The Eagles

It was just turning dark as Angus Davitt exited the trailer he and Sally had called home for the last six months. He picked up his net and cooler with the wheels on it and headed out of the campground on Stock Island. Angus walked the short distance to Route 1 past the boat yard. He glanced to his left across the small bridge separating him from Key West and turned right headed for the bridge at Boca Grande Pass where the water from the Bay flows into the Straights of Florida on the outgoing tide. The warm October sun was just setting. He had been doing this for months, timing his departure from the trailer before Sally got home from the jewelry store on Duval. He didn't want to talk.

When Angus got set up and removed from the department it was rough on Sally. She tolerated being at her job in town hall even though she was now isolated and shunned by her co-workers. Whether Angus had done something or nothing didn't matter. Political patronage is political patronage and that is how most got their jobs. They intended to keep those jobs and Sally went from being one of the gang to an outsider the night they set Angus up. When she and Angus took the buy-out the town offered they were worn down and looking for change. Jersey was suffering through February when they loaded up and headed as far south as they could go. When they hit Jacksonville they still had 8 hours to the Keys and that was just fine.

They lingered in Key Largo in the campground at the underwater park. They stopped for a few weeks at the K.O.A. campground on Sugarloaf Key and soaked up sunshine and warm water before driving the rest of the way into Key West. They kayaked the mangroves and hung out at the beach on the ocean side. They knew every bar on Duval and off Duval. If you can't chill in Key West it can't be done. Sally had had enough. It doesn't matter where you are it matters who you are. The trailer was getting way too small and Angus was getting way too close to being a Key's burn out. He was losing who he was. There was too much beer and too much down time. Sometimes the Keys will suck a man in and not let him out. He seemed content to stay on but she was done. She told Angus she was getting a job even though they didn't need the money. The first place she chose was a high end jewelry store. The second Sally walked through the door in her white sun dress and heals with her red hair done up real nice the owner knew opportunity when he saw it. She got all the hours she wanted and spent a lot of time dodging the advances of the owner and a large percentage of the male population she came in contact with. Angus either didn't notice or didn't care.

He could have taken the van to the bridge but he preferred to walk the half mile to his shrimping spot. He had knocked down one beer before he got there. He had been wearing the same pair of shorts and stained tee shirt for a week. He shaved only when Sally complained. The dust from the side of the road stuck to his feet and worn sandals. He stopped on the side of the concrete bridge, 15 feet above the water which was just beginning to flow toward the ocean. His net was 3'x3' with floats on the top and sinkers on the bottom. It had a bridle like a kite and he secured the line to the railing. The fishing was a waiting game. About the time he finished the second beer he shown his light into the net to see how many green eyes were looking back at him. He pulled in the net and dumped out his catch.
A couple of beers weren't enough to stop the thoughts, a broken record, over and over. He didn't know how to make it stop so he could move on. Sometimes the only way to see things clearly is to back off and remove yourself from the situation. Six months in paradise and it wasn't working.

Angus had never run from anything. He thought about the lost law enforcement job he loved, what had been home and Sally. He thought about the years of training and education that allowed him to move up the ranks and how it had all ended thanks to Chief Farquar. So why in the hell did Farquar pull the rug out from under him? No answers, no answers. After the third beer the thoughts would begin to fade.

ANYTIME ANYTHING ANYWHERE

Jimmy Buffett

When APBA decided to have the World Championships at Trump's Casino in Atlantic City, NJ in 1989, I don't think they realized what the New Jersey ocean was like in October. The U.I.M. international racing body ran the course with the APBA boats and a show it was. Between the international racers and the U.S. racers there were over a hundred boats. The concept was great; run right along the beach, boardwalk and casinos with a short leg out to sea. The milling area was in front of the inlet. Apparently whoever organized this thing didn't realize that the milling area, where we all had to wait for the race to start, was right where the waves outside the inlet were breaking. The weather was not cooperative. What a shock in New Jersey in October. There was a chance we could win this thing and I had one competitor in particular who could run with us in rough water. I didn't consider that he was from the Midwest. The sight of him standing on his driver's seat, head outside his canopy puking his guts out with a bad case of Mal De Mer as we throttled up for the start was gut wrenching. One down.

My driver was a guy with a motor lubricant company who I had throttled for all season. I had confidence in him as a driver but didn't know if he could take a pounding over 3 races like we were going to take. I had made up my mind this was the last race. My shoulder was shot from pulling g's while my hand was locked on the throttles for hours at a time with no arm support. I always pulled the belts down as tight as I could, but there were orange marks from my helmet on the inside of the f-16 canopy from bashing from side to side and my neck was never going to be the same. My right knee was giving me trouble, probably from bracing against the firewall all the time. The real problem was I was worn down mentally. The thrill was gone.

The headquarters and wet pits were at Trump's Taj Mahal. Trump knows how to throw a party. The private racer's parties were always high class, but the ones he threw at the Casino Hotel were special. My old dock mate Don Johnson, who didn't have a clue I shared a dock with him, was dating Melanie Griffith and they showed up along with the other cast of characters. The three race series was delayed by bad weather and we spent a lot of time hanging out.

Trump was a gracious host. We all had our uniform shirts on and so it was easy to identify who we were. He made the rounds followed closely by his own security people even though this was a private party up the stairs in a private ballroom away from the public. He worked his way around to me, looked me in the eyeballs and we were exchanging pleasantries when up the stairs came Stefano Casiraghi and his wife Princess Caroline of Monaco with a baby on her hip. I knew Casiraghi by reputation and we had been on the race course together in Key West a couple of times. Trump immediately turned and greeted them. All the while Trump was talking Casiraghi kept looking over at me. He excused himself as Donald was in mid-sentence, came over and stuck out his hand.

"You have that fantastic black boat with the fighter plane canopies, yes?"

"Yes, I do but you have a World Championship!"

"Would you let me sit in it?"

Well, yeah. What alternative universe have I entered? These people own Monaco. Stefano and I left Donald talking to Caroline and headed down the steps to the wet pits. He told me on the way that he was thinking of enclosing the cockpit on his boat, had seen the pictures of mine and now had a chance to see it first hand. He was considerably shorter than my driver, but I put a life jacket on the seat to raise him up and he belted in.

"This is the way to go. Many doing this now are putting the canopies straight onto the decks and I don't trust that."
I offered him a ride, but he declined and we went back to the party.

The following morning the show began in earnest. It had been arranged that Trump and his entourage would ride a boat down the line of race boats still in their slips and on signal, we would start the engines and follow him out past the gleaming white yacht, Trump Princess. We stood on the decks of our boats waving to him as instructed and Donald rode passed us in one of the largest go fast boats I had ever seen. I couldn't help but blurt out, "Did you ever get the feeling you were in the Colosseum and about to die for the Emperor." Cracked up my driver.

We had finished 4th and 5th in the first two races and the chances of us winning the Championship was zero to none. This last race was the roughest yet. We were flying south along the beach just outside the surfline in front of the spectators lining the boardwalk and casinos when Kevin Brown blew by us in his blue cat with the orange tipped bows. It was rough, really rough. We had a rough water boat and I felt we were on the edge and I had plenty of speed left but was unwilling to push harder. He passed us on the ocean side and I watched his boat dancing all over the place, running on the edge of control buffeted by unpredictable swells coming straight into our sides off an angry ocean. I lost him to sight in front of us, his location marked only by a helicopter flying above him. There arose from the surf a column of white water rising straight up toward the helicopter. By the time we got there nothing was showing of Kevin's boat other than the pickle fork orange bows bobbing pointed straight up at the sky. There was Angel One overhead and a rescue boat on the scene. We kept going.

The orange pillow where we would turn out to sea appeared ahead and I set the boat up for the driver to take the turn. Halfway into a hard left that had us taking the waves straight on all I heard over the intercom was, "steering's gone" before the boat snap rolled with me going over the top of the driver and the boat landing upside down. I remember every detail as though it was happening in slow motion:

We stayed strapped into our seats and the water was streaming over the canopies and I was aware we were still moving fast, wrong side up. I put my left hand on the cut out top of the canopy and my right hand on the belt release ready to free myself and exit underwater when the boat stopped. She didn't stop and I wasn't getting wet so I switched off the ignition switches in the hope I could save the motors. It was no more than 3 or 4 seconds when the boat snapped upright and the water poured off the canopy to reveal the yellow boat next to us with the side caved in. I understood instantly what had happened. When we went upside down our boat did a right angle 90 degree turn and came straight into the side of that boat. The impact flipped us right side up. We were still traveling plenty fast upside down when we hit the guy next to us. He was doing at least 80 mph coming out of the turn. The bow of Baby on my side pierced the side of the other boat 3 inches behind the heads of the riding crew and took out their firewall and fuel system. Three inches. So two objects are traveling parallel 50 feet apart at 80 mph. The one slightly ahead executes an uncontrolled 90 degree turn upside down and they collide. What was the margin for error between missing them by 3 inches or killing them on impact? I never was any good at math. We stopped moving and I told the driver to do nothing. I unbuckled, stood on the seat with my head outside the canopy and saw the throttles of the boat we had hit moving around and lifting the engine hatch. I yelled across, "Are you O.K.?" Richie flipped me the bird. Yeah you're O.K. The kicker was that we had been leading our class. I watched twelve boats pass us as we limped back to the inlet, me working one engine against the other to steer and the driver motionless and silent, I guess recovering from shock. I had planned this to be my last race anyway and it was.

Kevin Brown died on impact when the canopy meant to protect him came off the boat. Stefano Casiraghi won the VIM World Championship at that Trump race. He made Caroline a widow on October 3, 1990 when he raced again without converting his boat to a canopy cockpit.

I couldn't wait to leave Atlantic City. I was exhausted mentally and physically, but I think it was more the release I always get when I have ended something. The burden of the past is lifted and the future is endless and full of promise and new things. I left Baby with the pit crew, headed for my suite, took a quick shower, and had a car take me to Philadelphia for the flight back to Fort Lauderdale.

The prop plane from Lauderdale got me into Key West just after 11pm. I was glad I didn't know the driver Kate had sent for me. I was in no mood for small talk. The drive home was only 5 minutes. I asked the driver to drop me on the bridge on U.S. 1 at the north end of Stock Island and told him that I would walk home. He cracked something about "Don't jump" and I wondered if he had heard about my less than graceful exit from racing.

I stepped out onto the bridge at Boca Grand Pass to look into the peacefulness of the dark water. This was the end of one chapter in my life and I wanted to savor the feeling of coming down from it a little longer and start fresh tomorrow. I bit the end cap off one of my two remaining Cubans and took my time to carefully light it up. I had been vaguely aware of a tall, lanky figure with a cooler holding a line leading off the bridge. Now he spoke:

"That a Cuban? Nothin' in the world smells like a Cuban."

I walked toward him, "Yeah, you can smell the earth can't you?"

He grunted and I couldn't immediately determine if he regarded that statement as profound or if he labeled me an asshole. I offered him the other one.

"Only if you take a beer in return."

O.K., he had class. His demeanor conveyed that he was not a typical Key's burnout though he looked the part. I handed him the cigar and lighter and he took his time rolling the cigar in the flame and not drawing too hard so that he would have an even light. He knew how to light a fine cigar and I was glad I had given it to a guy who could appreciate it. I took his beer.

I had heard his accent right away and I put him from Jersey, somewhere north of the Raritan River, probably about exit 137 on the Parkway.

"You from Jersey?"

"Yeah, down here the last six months from the shore."
"You didn't grow up there though."

"No, born in Elizabeth and moved to Shoretown years ago."

"No shit? I grew up in Shoretown summers when I was a kid. Haven't seen it since the 60's."

"Before I got there", he said.

I watched him shine his light into the net the line was attached to. Staring back were the green eyes of the shrimp he was looking for. He was doing pretty good.

We got around to introducing ourselves. He held out his hand and said, "Angus Davitt". This was a man and his handshake showed it. The Cubans lasted close to 45 minutes. By that time we had cracked 3 beers a piece and the tide still had another hour left in it. He heard all about the boat company on Stock Island and how I got to Key West and why I had the car drop me off at the bridge. I heard about how he had been a cop and that he took an early retirement and was temporarily living in a trailer in the camp grounds on Stock Island until he decided what to do with the rest of his life.

He told me he was still too much Jersey and he was afraid he was losing his edge if he stayed here much longer. I told him I went the other way and didn't regret leaving Jersey for an instant. I asked him about being a cop and he told me about rising in the department and doing just about everything including the under cover work he liked the best. I lost track of the beers because the conversation was easy. He told me he wasn't much of a boat guy but loved the stories I told him about the racing circuit. I pulled the program from the Worlds at Atlantic City out of my carry on and he shown his headlamp on it while I fumbled through the pages to show him Baby. He took it from me and told me about how he used to watch the races in Point Pleasant and what a madhouse it was for the cops at that time. He paused on page 27 and brought the program closer for a better look. He asked if he could keep the program. I told him to go ahead, I had more. I didn't understand his haste as he pulled up the net, tossed the last of his catch into the cooler and headed off the bridge without saying anything. I followed him and he paused to let me catch up. We walked together to Stock Island. He turned into the camp ground. He went his way and I went mine. I half expected him to stop by the boat yard, but I never saw him on the Island again.

Angus got to the trailer about 1am, put the shrimp into the outside plug-in cooler, went in, stripped down and took a shower. Sally stirred as he slipped under the sheet and pressed against her back. He reached around for her breasts as he nuzzled her neck.

When they finished making love she stayed still to keep the feeling going for a few minutes. Then she climbed over him, threw his towel across her shoulder and he watched her, loving the view as she walked away down the hall.

"Can you be ready to leave tomorrow? We're going home."

"What took you so long?" she said, never looking back.

Angus woke to the sound of the trailer door opening and closing as Sally loaded the van. He dragged himself out of bed and made it to the kitchen where she had the coffee on. He barely kept up with her as she moved the last of their belongings for the 1,399 mile drive back to Shoretown. Angus was into the campground office as soon as it opened. He dumped the rest of the month's rent on the trailer, got back his deposit and they were driving past Boca Grande headed home by 9 that morning.

"Now would you like to tell me why you're in such a hurry? You've got 27 hours." And he did.

Angus drove straight through with purpose, switching off with Sally when he needed a break. They turned off the Parkway, drove to their neighborhood and pulled into their driveway early afternoon the following day. Angus was emptying the van while Sally turned on the heat and the house began to warm. She plugged in the remote wireless phone and put it into it's base to charge. Then she plugged in the police scanner, the one Angus always kept on even after he was off the job. He was carrying the stuff they had accumulated into the garage a few hours later when Sally called him into the house.
"Hurry up!"

"Listen to this," she said. Angus recognized the voice coming over the police scanner immediately.

It took him only a second longer to realize the voice wasn't a police radio. The voice was coming from a phone with a cordless hand set picked up by his scanner. The technology to separate the headset from the base unit of a telephone was patented in 1977 and cordless phones became a staple of American households. The base unit was still hard wired, but you could carry the handset up to a half mile from the base. The phones gave you the choice of 7 radio frequencies to choose from. If your neighbor was on one of them, you selected another so that your conversations didn't "step" on one another. Angus' scanner hit on a cordless phone that had to be within a half mile. Angus didn't wait. He went to Radio Shack and picked up a voice activated micro cassette tape recorder. He placed the scanner with the recorder touching it in the spare bedroom where there would be no noise from the house. He locked the scanner on the same frequency as the neighboring phone, and shut the door. Dead tired, they went to sleep.

Later that night Angus stirred briefly when he heard voices coming over the scanner too distant from his bed to make out clearly. He knew the voice activated tape recorder he had placed next to the scanner would click on. Simple: The scanner was set to the frequency of that phone. The voice activated micro cassette recorder collected the conversation and Angus could listen to it anytime he wanted. He smiled at the irony of now having access to Chief Farquar's phone conversations and he went back to sleep. Careless conversation through the air was not a wire tap. Anything he recorded could be used. Over the next weeks the micro cassettes made their way to the shoe box he kept in the attic. He and Sally never used their own cordless phone again.

THE FIRE STILL BURNS
Miami Vice/ Russ Ballard

The Church had always played a large part in the lives of Angus and Sally's Irish immigrant family. The two still had many true friends there. Sally caught up with her girlfriends and Angus called Father James. Father was not only his priest of choice, but his friend. When he was a cop it was not unusual for Angus to stop in to see Father James when he was on the road at night. The priest always had a cup of coffee and a good conversation. Father James was beloved, a priest who always had a kind word and concern for anybody and who was never without a smile. His reputation as a trusted confidant provided him with plenty of opportunities to serve and he did. Everybody in the parish knew the story of Father James and how he had been wounded in Vietnam while taking mass to the boys in the field somewhere up near the DMZ. The scar on his forehead, below his hairline, was visible. He walked with a slight limp. The shrapnel pieces they left in his body surfaced on occasion and he went to the V.A. in New York to have them removed. He often told how being wounded had brought him closer to God.

The day he got blown up he had been carted out on the same chopper he came in on, blue body bags around him and a needle putting blood back into his body until they got him to a field hospital. He spent several weeks there until they could get him stabilized. The field surgeon had done a good job. He managed to save the leg but the recovery and physical therapy took close to a year in a series of stateside hospitals ending with a stay in New York. When he was released from the V.A. the Trenton Diocese gave Father the assignment he wanted. He took the assistant pastorship in Shoretown. It was not promised, but intimated, that he would be named senior pastor when Father Gambina retired. He was still waiting.

Father James met Angus at the back door of the Rectory. His room was first on the right and he had prepared a one pot meal for the two of them. Father opened the door and gave Angus a hug. Angus looked over Father's shoulder down the long hall and up the stairs into the dining room. Father Gambina was sitting alone at a massive solid oak table big enough to seat 8, the housekeeper pouring his wine as he ate. Gambina had been at this church a long time. He was old school. With his priest collar came an air of authority that set him apart from his flock. The Monsignor could count on him to parrot the line Rome dictated. He believed the mystery of the church was vital to maintain control and he lived a life of contentment and peace, rigid and unwilling to change. He served from the altar acting out the high mass in Latin with rigid authority and left confession and counseling to his assistant Father James. Father turned right into his room and Angus followed.

Father Jame's room reminded Angus of a hotel room. There was a single bed. He had a desk placed by the window looking into the parking lot and a bookcase on the longest wall. Next to the bookcase Father had positioned a cabinet with a fold down front that became a counter. This was his kitchen in which he stored two place settings, a two burner electric hot plate, a fry pan and a pot with a lid and utensils. On the top of the cabinet against the wall were wine glasses and coffee cups. The bottom portion of the cabinet held the coffee, food and bottles of wine. He had two folding chairs to position on either side of the folded down counter and his cooking counter became his dining table. The bathroom was little more than the essentials with a stall shower. His recliner was positioned to look out the window and his goose neck reading light often burned long into the night. This was home.

After Father had shut the door and they were alone Angus asked, "Do you ever eat with him?"

"He doesn't ask me very often, but sometimes. Anyway, I like my own cooking."

Father had prepared his one pot paella that he knew was Angus' favorite. The loaf of bread from the bakery across the street capped it off. They got into the second bottle of wine before dinner was finished and the conversation flowed just as freely. Angus got Father caught up on Key's life. When Father asked him what brought him back without warning Angus was unwilling to tell him more than "it was time" to get back to a normal life. "Anyway, you're not in the Keys Father and I missed your cooking." Father had never doubted that Angus was set up and pushed out of the department. His trust and friendship never wavered and Angus was grateful for that. Father had spent hours with him going back over the events leading to the set up, but he was just as perplexed as Angus. Right after the incident the police chief Farquar left his church and moved to the church on the other side of town even though he didn't live in that parish. Father pondered.

While he was recovering from his wounds 20 years ago Father had plenty of time for contemplation and study while he bounced around hospitals. He devoted himself to a better understanding of human nature to the point where he added a degree in Sociology to his education. By the time he got to the parish he was a licensed counselor in NJ. Angus knew that aside from his mission of offering the gift of eternal life through Christ, this was the most important way in which he served. Father often ran things by Angus, particularly when he wanted a lay opinion or needed a secular view point. In every case he was careful to not reveal any details that would give a hint as to who he was talking about. Angus asked him how the counseling was going. Father gave him a run down on the usual problems he was helping people deal with looking away as he talked, searching for a summation. Then he turned to face Angus directly and his face hardened.

"I have counseled several divorcing couples. But I have a particularly bad situation going on now. The wife has confided in me, poor thing, and her situation goes way beyond what is moral, ethical or legal."

Father went on the explain that her lawyer had forced her into a sexual relationship and that she was being used and saw no way out. Of course Father offered no names and made no reference to anything that would give Angus the slightest clue who he was talking about. Father was clearly angry and frustrated. As her priest and her counselor he could not go to the authorities. She would not have allowed it anyway. Shoretown was way too small to live with the humiliation plus she had a nine year old daughter to whom she would have to explain. On top of that, the divorce was still on-going and she had no money. Anger was an emotion he rarely felt and Angus had never seen him like this. All Angus could do was provide an ear to which Father could vent and the counselor became the counseled. This was a 2 bottle of wine night after which Angus went home.

The next morning he placed a call to Rocco Rinaldi, the guy who had built his house.

"Hey, Rocco, I am back in town and I have some work for you."

Rocco Rinaldo had begun to scout out Shoretown as a place to move to soon after the Newark riots, which affected not only Newark, but all of Essex County. His shop, and Calvin's home, was located in West Orange directly behind the Thomas Edison complex on Main Street where the great inventor did much of his work. The complex, now a museum, backs up directly to Orange. It faces Main Street which forms a dividing line between Orange and the hills rising into West Orange. Rocco's shop and equipment yard was sandwiched between Edison and Orange on the wrong side of the line. Edison's home was in Llewelyn Park which was only a mile south on Main Street. The Park is one of the oldest planned communities in the

U.S. and traces to 1853 when the Oranges were becoming one of the most prestigious cities in the country. It is a gated, protected, bucolic enclave of parkland and magnificent homes climbing and sprawling in natural beauty up the east side of the West Orange mountain. It has been home to some of the most successful people in the U.S. Only 12 miles from Manhattan it remains so today. Seven Oaks section of Orange was slightly less affluent and located east, closer to Newark, south toward South Orange. With no barrier to the inner city decay Seven Oaks property values plummeted as did the formerly magnificent mansions and apartment buildings in East Orange. Who knew how far west the crime and poverty pushing on Rocco would spread? He thought a lot about making the move south. He did a lot of his contemplating at the Pour House on Main Street 1/4 mile from his shop. This was the same bar that was the favorite watering hole of the Kelly astronaut twins, though Rocco proceeded them by a decade.

Rocco was holding up his third glass of Crown Royal, neat, admiring the warm color and peering into it as though the glass were a crystal ball ready to unlock some great secret. He was lost in the thoughts running through his head.

"Are you going to stare at it or drink it?", came a voice filled with warmth even though sarcastic.

Rocco turned slowly and as he lowered his glass her face appeared. A single black curl hung down over one eye and she brushed it aside as she leaned toward him. He was looking into the face of Renee, a cheerleader from high school. She was as confident, outgoing and sure of herself as he was shy. In high school he never dated but he found himself staring at her back then and not getting caught because she was always on stage and he was one of many.

He answered, "I was thinking about leaving after this one, but maybe I'll stay." (Where did that come from????), he wondered.
"Good choice", she said. "I've been at the end of the bar. My friends from work left and I wanted to ask if you were Rocco who played hockey in high school."

He found himself fully engaged in conversation with a woman who was one of the most popular girls in school, whom he would not have dared talk to a few years before. It amazed him that the conversation was this easy and that he kept her smiling and time had no meaning.

Renee suggested they grab something to eat and the evening was one of those where you don't know how it got to be 11pm on a week night, but it was.

"Let's put something on the jukebox and then call it a night", said Renee. She walked him over and plugged a dime. "I like this one", she said.

The metal arm moved to the record, grabbed it and placed it on the turntable. D-9, 'Let's Spend The Night Together' started to turn. Renee took Rocco by the hand and led him back to the bar where she picked up the tab and they left to the Stones:

"Oh, you know I'm smiling baby you need some guiding baby I'm just deciding baby Let's spend the night together Now I need you more than ever Let's spend the night together now."

There are some men who just need the right woman to give them a push. There are some women who just want a good man.

Rocco recognized that business opportunity and quality of life was 60 miles south and he wanted to grow with it, he and a hundred thousand others from North Jersey who learned how far south they were by parkway exit number. Renee had no trouble transferring from the bank branch she managed in West Orange to one at the shore, but they took 2 years to put the pieces in place. Rocco's strong financials allowed him to establish a banking relationship down there and building material suppliers were sprouting up all over the place. Rocco bought his first piece of sand and scrub pine trees in 1971. The tract was a little ways west of town, away from the water, but close enough to sell the four houses he planned to build. He split his work between North Jersey and South Jersey for two years depending on Calvin to ramrod the North Jersey jobs while he finished off the houses to the south. It was not unusual for him to begin in West Orange with Calvin at 6am in order to have the equipment and supplies ready when the crew came in. Then he would head south for the one hour commute in time to be on the job at 8 when the framers arrived. He ramrodded that project until the sun went down and then he drove back an hour north at night. 12 hour days were easy with Renee waiting home after work. Renee understood and never worried.

When he phased out the shop in West Orange in 1976 he offered a job to any of the guys working for him who wanted to relocate. All but one took him up on it. He kept his college educated Office Manager and hired a Project Manager with a B.A. in business. Building homes expanded into large infrastructure projects and an engineer moved into the office. By 1980 Rocco was spending his time doing what he liked best, getting dirty playing on his heavy equipment and using his vision to see possibility where others saw nothing. He left the book stuff to his staff and did what good administrators always do. He gave them a project, told them what he expected, gave them the tools to do it and held them accountable for the results.

By 1980 Calvin was beginning to show his age. His tall frame was weakening and pitching him forward. His hair was white and made a stark contrast with his black skin. He was still strong as a man his age could be. He was simply physically worn down. He was also happier than be had ever been. He pulled himself up the railing to his spacious 3 room apartment. The library he had always dreamed of faced the equipment yard and had a big picture window on the outside wall. That way he could keep an eye on what was going on. He never quit being a patient mentor. He was on site and his door was open 24/7. New employees were always assigned to him and he made sure they did things the "G and R" way. They were his children and they came to him often for advice or to just hang out with the mentor. Long, dark walnut book shelves lined the interior wall of Calvin's Library. On the center shelf dead middle stood one book. He had taken the two pictures he had of his mother out of her Bible and placed them in frames on either side to hold the tired old book up. The shelves to the right held every manual for every piece of equipment he and Rocco owned. The book cases on either side held every book he had ever read. He had discovered the classics and had a set of the great philosophers done in sumptuous green leather, the first real extravagance he had ever allowed himself. A matching set of the great writers beginning with Dante waited patiently. The only piece of furniture in his sanctuary was a reclining reading chair with a side table and a green shaded library lamp.

Calvin, the never married southern transplant, added grandchildren to his family. Rocco's twin boys called him "Poppa". They had known him their whole lives and when Rocco took them to the construction yard they took a direct path to Poppa's apartment. They wouldn't leave until he read to them. For a while Shell Silverstein's "Where The Sidewalk Ends" was their favorite. That gave way to "The Magic School Bus" series along with "Goosebumps" and "Where The Wild Things Are". He gave the readings all he had and delighted in their reactions to his theatrics.

Then came the Sunday morning Rocco asked Calvin if he wanted to go with him and Renee to Father Jame's mass. After it was over Renee asked Calvin what he thought. The southern baptist fundamentalist told her that he found a peacefulness and holiness about that man. "God lives in him", was the way Calvin put it. Renee looked forward to putting the two together at the dinner following mass the next Sunday. Dinner with Rocco and Renee and Calvin and James became a cherished tradition. At that first dinner Renee got the ball rolling by asking Calvin what he thought of the mass.

"Doesn't matter whose church it is if God lives there. God only lives there if he lives in the preacher."

Then Calvin told them the story of an old homeless man who was going from city to city. He camped out under an underpass outside of this particular town and they knew he was there and they left him alone. He ventured into town on Sunday mornings when the stores were closed and the streets were quiet. He would put on the second shirt and pair of pants he owned that he had carefully washed in the creek by the underpass and make himself as clean and presentable as he could. He wandered around the quiet peaceful streets. He enjoyed the peacefulness of the town green, big enough to be a park. Being the heart of the town it was surrounded by the finest buildings and a massive stone church built over a hundred years ago. He watched the parishioners drive up in their fancy cars all dressed up and looking good and he saw the welcoming committee at the door. He heard the music and the singing and one morning he got up the courage to go. A smiling greeter wearing a white carnation on his dark suit recognized him and met him at the door. "I am afraid the church is full and there is no more room." The old man said nothing, he simply looked at him imploringly. The greeter weakened and went on, "Why don't you go on over to the park and do some praying and I am sure you will be talking to God just fine. After the service, come on back and you can come in for a few minutes. "The old man turned and did just that. After the service the old man watched the congregation leave one at time and each shake the Pastor's hand as they left. The parade took a long time. The old man left the peaceful park and walked down the sidewalk back toward his camp. The greeter was closing the door to lock up when he saw the old man. "Come on in old timer you can stay for a few minutes while we clean up." The drifter walked to him, looked him in his eyes and said, "I did what you suggested. I went into the park and I prayed and I marveled at his creations and God reached out to me. He told me he doesn't live in your church and I don't have to go in there to find him. Thank you anyway."

Calvin went on, "I have been forced to ask myself why an almighty, all knowing creator, who can do anything it wants to do, would reveal itself to only one group of people at only one point in history? Wouldn't it reveal itself to different peoples in a way their culture would understand? God's core message is the same in all religions. That is until man gets hold of it and corrupts it for his own purpose. God either lives in a man or it doesn't. That's the problem with the world today. Too many people sayin' 'My god is better than your god' and dressing different so they can create a division among men. Doesn't matter what religion Christian, Jew, Muslim, Buddhist, Hindu or anything else, if it claims it is the only way to see God then it serves man, not God. I found God through Christ so Christ is my savior and my God is Christ's God. It is a God of love not hate. I sometimes wonder what happened to Christ's mission: Tear down the temple system that was enriching the priests and government and make religious worship available to anyone so that they can see the kingdom of God. Got himself killed because of that. His teachings of kindness and inclusion for everyone who seeks to worship get lost. Organized religion is either a window or a wall. You gotta look close at who's doing the preaching."

Rocco and Renee sat back and soaked it in.

Father James played devil's advocate, a strange position to take for one with as much faith as he had, but the discussion was getting good and he wanted to keep it going.

"Ah Calvin, it appears you believe spirituality is a creation of God and religion is a creation of man. You have defined God as being a loving being bringing people together. Seems to me he is more complicated then that. The Bible is full of God acting in ways that are not always loving and sometimes appear to be downright cruel."

Calvin responded, "Depends on who wrote that part of the Bible and what they really meant. The Good Book is full of metaphors and parables. You have to mine it like you enter a gold mine and look for nuggets within the dirt. You and I both know, Father, that the Bible as we know it is an assembled group of writings put together by your Roman Church with an agenda, no offense."

Father knew that of course Calvin was right. Constantine, the pagan Roman Emperor, who converted to Christianity, commissioned the Council of Nicaea in the 4th century to assemble the Book. His goal was to unify the Empire's religious factions. This he did by ordering and paying for it's creation. The creators of the Bible, under his direction, selected and edited various old texts. They included the ones that supported their position and they discarded those that didn't. Many of the inclusions were in the "Coptic" language and had to be translated. The translations were only as good as the scribes doing the translating and the inclusions only made it if they supported the position of the newly created unified Church.

Father answered, "But you have to admit that God's divine hand guided them."

"I would Father, but a wise man always questions motive." Calvin went on, "How would you explain the Dead Sea Scrolls? They were not found until 1947 and are unaltered from the time they were written, about the same time as the Gospels that made it into the Bible. They have not undergone the changes that the Bible has over the years and they present a different view of Christ in which, it can be argued, he is not viewed as divine at all but as prophet. And surely you have read the Gnostic Gospels, the books that didn't make it?"

This was getting good and Father was too secure in his faith to not continue. "So Calvin, what is it you believe about Christ?"

"I worship the God that brought Christ the Preacher to man. He walked the walk and talked the talk that can bring us all together. Doesn't mean I think his way is the only way to overcome the evil that tortures men on this earth. I believe the worst sin is to use the name of any god as an excuse to amass power and wealth and to control others. Religion is responsible for more pain and suffering and inhumanity than any other force on earth." Calvin was careful to not make any direct reference to the Roman Catholic Church, but it was not lost on Father.

"Calvin it always conflicted me when I thought about two armies staring across at each other and each invoking their god to give them the strength to overcome the other guy's god."

Father spoke this from the heart.

"You know Father that my God, your God, lives within me and he lives within you. I recognized that about you right away. Our's is the God of grace and mercy. No church can change him. No preacher can twist him. Any strength we have comes from the fact he lives in us. I could never worship a god who doesn't want to bring mankind together and neither could you."

Calvin raised his wine glass to Father signaling that he was ending their discussion, content that Father understood he felt their connection. Father's glass met him halfway and they looked into each others' eyes needing to say nothing else.

On one particular Sunday Father James let Calvin depart and then he spoke to Rocco.

"I have tickets to see the play "Nunsense", been wanting to see it for years. You and Renee like to see it with me?" Renee jumped at the chance to go to New York and sealed the deal for Rocco.
"Can you drive? I need to stop at West 64th before we head downtown to the matinee."

Most who knew the priest knew he spent his days off in New York City. Most thought he went to the V.A. That Wednesday Rocco drove Father through the Lincoln Tunnel and up 10th Avenue to an apartment house on the West Side overlooking Riverside Drive. They waited while Father entered the building and emerged a minute later with Sylvia.

"Holy crap, we're pimping for a priest!", was what came out of Renee's mouth.

When Father James was blown off his feet that day in Vietnam he joined the other 303,643 American soldiers wounded during the conflict. The doctors did the best they could and sent him home and into the Veteran's Hospital System in New York City to complete his recovery. His head trauma was superficial and the gash from which he lost a lot of blood healed into a four inch scar between his eyebrow and hairline. The soft tissue on the rest of his body absorbed more pieces, but his leg took the worst hit. The field surgeon did a great job. The medic with the chopper had carefully aligned the lower part of the leg with the break mid-thigh and splinted it. The shrapnel missed the femoral artery by an inch or this story of Father would have ended right there on a dusty airstrip. The surgeon at the field hospital re-attached ligaments, tendon and muscle and Father kept his leg.

Only the victim of trauma knows it's affect on the mind. Father found his return to the U.S. was bittersweet. His service had been almost non-existent. He wasn't angry and he wasn't sad. He didn't bargain with God to restore him physically. As he lay in that bed he became even more resolute in his belief that God had plans for him. He had been marked and physically maimed and he found that strangely liberating. He had a new found calmness that comes from acceptance and a new taste for life. He was anxious to move forward.

At the hospital he was captive. When they first brought him in he went under the knife one more time to fine tune the field surgeon's repair. Assured he would keep the leg, they let him rest until he healed sufficiently to begin physical therapy. In Vietnam the hospital had been an assembly line of wounded and maimed with nurses moving down the rows of beds placed within a few feet of each other.

Assembly lines are impersonal no matter how well intended.

From the day Father was placed in the hospital bed until the day he was discharged months later, a young nurse tended him. Sylvia had graduated nursing school only a month before Father arrived. When she entered his room the first time she felt an aura that drew her in. In spite of her age she was not inexperienced nor was she naive. She was confident and unguarded and soon found herself in the presence of a mentor with whom she lusted for deep conversations about life. He made her think, he challenged her intellect and over time he revealed himself as a man.

Rocco and his wife did not say a word to each other as Father and Sylvia approached the car. Her black hair was cut just above her shoulders and her green eyes came to life as Father introduced her as the nurse that had cared for him when he returned home years ago. The drive downtown was filled with conversation that never once touched on their relationship. She was direct and energetic and open and they watched the affect it had on Father who shifted into a higher gear when the two were talking one on one. Her conversation with them was easy and she obviously didn't care that he was a priest. Her hand rested on his thigh and he covered it with his own and that is how they rode downtown to the theater. After the play they had dinner at Top of The Sixes with Manhattan lit up below them. As Rocco pulled the car up to the apartment Sylvia thanked them and she and Father walked in hand and hand. Father would find his own way home.

FORBIDDEN LOVE

Madonna

Karl Pederson was on the fast track out of New England the day he learned he had completed all his requirements for graduation. They could mail him his diploma. He had two wishes: The first was that his father get him out of the draft lottery and the second was that he stop needing his father's help. He needed the old man for 3 more years and then he could accomplish what he really wanted and claim it as his own. There was nothing more important then acquiring wealth. He grew up in the best house in the neighborhood and had the first car. College had been easy. Mr. Pederson provided the money that set him apart. He liked the way this felt and looking down from whatever perch he chose was how he wanted his life.

His father made one call to a lawyer friend who was head of the draft board and Karl was issued another student deferment. He found the only accelerated law school in New Jersey and cut law school from 3 to 2 years. Another phone call by his father and he was clerking for the Superior Court Judge of the Family Court. His father was a defense attorney, well known for taking on some of the sleaziest clients in Essex County. It paid very well. But Karl recognized that it took too much work.

Trial work took too much preparation. Sure the billable hours were great but there was little room for not actually putting in the time. He couldn't comprehend a general practice, closing real estate, writing wills, etc. There was nothing there to separate him from the pack. His year spent clerking in Family Court convinced him that for the right kind of a lawyer divorce was a door to opportunity.

He watched lawyer after lawyer come into court trailing wheeled carts loaded down with files that translated into billable hours. He watched them burn hours standing around the court house with their clients in order to be heard for 5 minutes on a simple motion or meet with another lawyer appointed by the judge to mediate a dispute. Actually working in a trial setting was to be avoided if at all possible. Billable hours was how the game was played and working it was a legal industry.

In 1969 Elizabeth Kubler-Ross, a Swiss American Psychiatrist, developed a five stage emotional response to loss. Denial, anger, bargaining, depression and acceptance were identified. She never meant them to be a linear progression. There are many types of loss that result in grief and each individual experiences loss in their own way. Loss does not have to be from a death. Grief can be felt from losing a job, moving away from friends and family or simply losing a way of life. Not everyone feels the stages the same way. Some visit none of them. Some visit all of them. Some experience them out of order or add nuances and shades not readily definable. Kubler Ross raised awareness and opened the door for kindness and understanding by providing a basic road map for those on a journey of grief. Divorce is a study in grief and Karl recognized this as a useful tool. It would take years for him to polish his technique.

When he finished his clerkship in Essex County he left behind the antiquated building overlooking the desolation of once proud Newark and made his way south to Shoretown. He joined the population explosion and he was on the ground floor. He would have liked to hit a home run right away, but that would have meant going to work for an existing law firm and that would have placed him in a subservient position. He had his own ideas about how to be successful on his own terms.

Initially he played the game straight and developed a reputation as a family court lawyer. He was one of the first in the area and he grew with the system. Judges and lawyers met at a watering hole called "The Bar". They drank after work and they did what business people do. Alliances were formed, pecking orders established and deals made. The Bar became the hang out for anybody who was anybody in business. They joined the Chamber of Commerce and Rotary and The Lions.

Karl perfected his control and manipulation. Most of his clients were on their first divorce. Ignorance of how the game is played was extremely profitable. He realized that divorce is fertile ground for emotion. He also realized that rarely are a divorcing couple at the same place emotionally. It was likely the one initiating the divorce wanted out in a hurry while the other was trying to come to grips with the situation. He got to know a client intimately while they spilled their guts about their, or their spouse's, transgressions real or imagined. A client's denial that the spouse wanted a divorce was only one of the markers he could use to identify a client ripe for picking. This would be a long road. What he really liked was anger. Once a client accepted the divorce was going to happen he could convince them he would fight to get them what they deserved. This was about the division of property, money, houses, assets, income lost, income stolen, future income and the division of children. As long as he kept his eye on the ball, children were property. What was he supposed to be a damn grief counselor? He had someone for that job.

Within a couple of years he had his formula perfected. He gathered intelligence at the first free consultation. He weeded out the clients that would not generate the most profit. This served him well because he developed a reputation for taking high profile cases as well as guaranteeing a substantial income for himself. This he accomplished by having the potential client fill out a "case information statement" defining assets and income of both parties. If he took them on he never had them pay a retainer or sign a retainer agreement. It was all about trust between client and attorney, wasn't it?

He knew the other attorneys who would play the divorce game and he would recommend one of them if his client could pass it on to the spouse.

This began the exchange of letters. Attorney "A" would write letter "1" which would generate letter "2" from the opposing attorney's secretary. If the opposing spouse had chosen an attorney not in the divorce industry, no matter. If there wasn't the potential for substantial profit he would simply hand the client off to someone else.

He then assessed whether or not his client needed "counseling" to help deal with the emotions of this loss. He kept a "counselor" on the side. She had an online sociology degree and was licensed to practice family counseling. It did not take her long to realize if she could keep a client in "anger" her billable hours added up and so did Karl's. The tricky part was to bring the client out of anger to "resolution" so that Karl could end the case when he needed to. The need to end a case became evident when the assets of the clients ran out or there was the potential to have to go into court for a protracted period of time. What was not explained to the client was that existing Case Law dictated practically every scenario for the division of property. Karl was a fraud. Beyond that he was a sociopath.

Over time Karl developed the template for his perfect client: She was a naive, not business savvy woman, who needed emotional support to walk her through the divorce from a husband with plenty of assets. Hopefully the husband was represented by one of the other family law specialists who knew how to play the game and was willing. Children provided leverage and complications that took time and money to straighten out. Karl enjoyed thinking about how well he could select a victim. A naive woman, no matter how intelligent, was an opportunity for him to complete the perfect score. His technique was simple: Develop trust, create emotional and legal dependency, strip away the assets and her ability to pay and she was ready for his final act of betrayal. He set aside Saturday mornings for "special" client meetings. His staff was not in the office. Very few other professional offices in his building were open. Faced with no way to defend herself the conquest was easy. A reassuring word that he would make sure he took care of her until the divorce was over, in spite of her inability to pay him now, was usually all it took to get her onto her knees. The orgasms he had during sex with his wife could not compare to what he felt those Saturday mornings.

Father James had seen little of Karl even though they both now lived in

Shoretown. Their connection from the old days in West Orange was tenuous. Father had his number, having witnessed how Karl manipulated others first hand. Karl knew one of his current clients/victims had changed counselors and left the counselor he could control, but he didn't know she had gone to Father James. Father rarely went to The Bar, but that particular late afternoon Angus took him there. They had a couple glasses of wine by the time court shut down for the day and a few of the lawyers hit their watering hole. Karl Pederson was one of them. Father saw him enter and his anger was immediate. He brought the wine to his lips and held it there for a long time as he looked past the glass at a man for whom he had only contempt. He composed himself and his thoughts and he knew opportunity.

"Come on Angus, I want to introduce you to somebody."

They got up and approached Karl who was talking to a group of lawyers.

"Hello Karl, meet Angus Davitt." Karl knew of Angus and his problems with the town but he had never met the man. Angus introduced himself and they exchanged a few words. Father told Angus he would meet him back at the table and turned, smiling to Karl.

"Come on down to the end of the bar. I'll buy you a drink for old times sake." Karl followed.

Father placed his back to the wall at the end of the bar and signaled the bartender for another round. He looked past Karl who had his back to the room to be sure no one was within hearing range. Karl smiled and began to speak but Father Jame's face turned hard and Father cut him off like a machete slicing through a blade of grass.
"Listen, you son of a bitch, I know how you operate and I know one of your clients who you fuck every Saturday morning. I have no regard for you or anyone like you. If you died today there would be one less piece of shit on earth. You will stop using her and you will hand her off to another lawyer whom I will approve or I will make sure the right people know about your game."

Karl was stunned but recovered enough to begin to try to intimidate the priest. Father cut him off again and continued, "Everyone looking sees me smiling as I buy you a drink and we are talking. I would suggest you keep it that way. From what I can see you are a serial rapist. I have prayed that one woman, just one, come forward. If one would so would others. You walk a very thin line and some day it will happen. Keep looking behind you for the one who will or the husband who will find out and take care of you himself. For now do what I say and set her free. One day I will sprinkle Holy Water on your grave and pray God grants you absolution from your sins and gives you eternal grace. Then I will piss on it." Father smiled, said loudly "Enjoy your drink Karl, good to see you." and he returned to Angus.

"He didn't look too happy. What was that about?" "Just my attempt to save another soul Angus. Let's head out."

Angus dropped Father off at the Rectory. As Father entered the phone was ringing and he took a call from Sylvia that would change his life.

Angus drove straight home and went directly to the shoe box full of tapes he had recorded off the careless cordless phone. It took him 15 minutes to find a tape of Chief Farquar talking to the voice he had heard minutes ago, a voice on several of the tapes. He listened several times to one brief phone call to be sure he was right. Angus asked himself the question, "Why was it that Karl Pederson and Chief Farquar spoke on the phone only periodically about who was having pizza delivered to whom?"

I GOT ALL YOU NEED

Willie Dixon /Joe Bonamassa

The Genovese organized crime family had a huge presence in North Jersey under the leadership of the Boiarados who ruled from their estate in Livingston, just over the second mountain abutting West Orange. They had their fingers anywhere they could make money. After they picked Newark clean there was the docks, trucking, construction, loan sharking, you name it they had their hands in it.

In 1976 New Jersey allowed gambling in Atlantic City. This added to the migration of population from north to south via the Garden State Parkway. The shore area began at the Raritan Bridges where you could exit and head due east toward Sandy Hook. This was the Jersey-side entrance to New

York Harbor, the only harbor in the U.S. marked by "twin" light houses set high up on the cliffs. The light house was situated at the site of Marconi's radio tower from which the first trans-Atlantic radio transmission in history was made.

The Twin Lights looked down on the Highlands which was home to Vito Genovese who founded the powerful family. He brought with him James "Little Pussy" Russo who was noted for running a loansharking and bookmaking operation out of a drug store in the West Orange valley. You could tell when business was open by his pink Cadillac convertible parked in front. The Newark cops had given him his nickname, "Little Pussycat", because he was an adept cat burglar. "Big Pussy" was already taken by his older brother who was another "made man".

Pussy lived in Long Branch in an apartment in The Harbor Island Spa and was conspicuous by his habit of riding around the Shore, top down, radio blaring in shear enjoyment of his mobdum and ability to intimidate. His flamboyance apparently didn't sit to well with the big boys. He was picked up by FBI surveillance telling another made man to stay away from Boiardo's estate in Livingston because that is where men were taken to be killed. Pussy said that he, personally, had dragged a dead body to the crematory. On the evening of April 26, 1979 "Little Pussy" Russo entertained guests. They shot him in the head three times with a .32 caliber and missed with one shot from a .38. He fell among the stuffed cats he surrounded himself with. The assassins took their time to lock the door so he wouldn't be found right away and departed. He was found the next morning.

The cops may have left Angus, but Angus never stopped being a cop. He was aware of the mob presence at the Jersey Shore. One of the characters he knew lived in the area was James, "Jimmy The Brush" Fyfe. Fyfe hung out between Atlantic City, Seaside and southern Monmouth County. He lived only a mile from Angus and was frequently seen around the area bars.

Angus had tried, since the night he was set up and accused of taking money from a prisoner, to figure out why. He knew Chief Farquar was in on it of course, but he had no idea how high or to whom it went. He had kept his nose out of politics. That might not get him promoted, but there was no reason why it would get him fired. The Mayor and Business Administrator had seemed to treat him fairly during the buy-out negotiations. The town attorney was a "stand up" guy and even seemed remorseful about the whole leave-the-department-buy-out-thing, although of course, he couldn't express it. Anyone with skin in the game had distanced themselves from him and there were no leads he could find anywhere. For months he had replayed every day leading up to the night of the set up searching his memory for anything out of the ordinary.

The night Angus had that chance meeting on the bridge outside Key West was an epiphany. The picture in the race program from Marathon jumped off the page the instant he saw it. The Point Pleasant, New Jersey race had been big that previous summer. The boats began arriving in town a couple of days ahead. There were the usual driver's v.i.p. parties, the radio interviews and the parade through Point Pleasant complete with the Budweiser Clydesdales and an air show by The Blue Angels. The events took place in Point Pleasant but there was the usual spill over into the surrounding towns. Angus recalled his duty assignment that night, two days before the race. He was inside in command of the night shift. It was a peaceful night. Many of the boat crews stayed in the hotels in Shoretown, but the parties were in Point and the bars and boardwalk there were packed. He replayed that night in his mind:

About 11pm Angus left the station in charge of the other sergeant for a few minutes to get some fresh air and to run down to the mall to pick up a pizza before they closed. He took an unmarked car and drove the short distance, using the side entrance into the mall. He noticed a truck pulled up to the back door of Tony's place. What caught his attention was the picture of the race boat on the side of the big box. "Majestic" one of the bigger cats, was painted in her war colors and spanned the whole side of the truck. He continued around to the front and his headlights shown directly through the front door of the pizza joint. The sign on the door was turned to "closed" and he cursed to himself that he was 5 minutes too late. He went to the door and knocked. Tony came around the corner of the counter and talked to him through the glass door. He saw no one else.

"We're closed Angus," "You got a slice at least?" "Naw, the ovens are off, we're closed," "What about the truck out back?" "Yeah, they called in an order and they got the last pie. Can't do nothin' for you tonight."

Angus left just as "Majestic" pulled out from behind the store. He turned out onto the main road directly behind them and didn't bother to pass for a half mile until the truck turned into a hotel parking lot. He continued on to the station.

After meeting the race boat driver on the bridge in Key West and seeing the race program with the boat picture, he replayed that night on the walk from the bridge to his trailer and he thought like a cop. Why was the race boat truck around the back? Then he remembered the loading door of the truck was pointed at the rear door of the pizza joint. Why hadn't they pulled the truck cab straight in? Would Tony have opened the back door for a pizza pick up? Did he know those guys? When he followed the truck up the road did they think the Crown Vic was following them? The questions mounted and he needed the contacts he had back home in Jersey.

Angus had many friends in law enforcement on the county level. He had been in Shoretown a long time and those guys knew him. The word he got was that none of them believed he was guilty of anything. But they knew how the game was played. If the politicians wanted you out you were out. Angus called up a friend in the prosecutor's office the day he got back. They met over a beer down in Bayville, well south of Shoretown. Angus laid it out for the detective and asked for his help to get background on Majestic and on Tony and the pizza joint. Angus couldn't shake the thought that none of that should have taken place. The only explanation was that he was in the wrong place at the wrong time and Tony got spooked. Maybe the guys in the truck thought he was tailing them. Didn't matter. This was the only lead he had and he was going to run it into the ground.

It took about a week and what came back peaked his interest. APBA supplied some answers about the boats history. Majestic had raced under a different name and had been owned by Willie Falcone, currently in jail for smuggling vast quantities of cocaine. She had been purchased by a guy new to the national racing circuit who lived on Staten Island. When she wasn't racing she was stored at a boatyard in Homestead, Florida that specialized in go-fast boats. Her owner was not listed as part of the riding crew. In the three years she had been racing under this name she only ran one of the three Florida races, Marathon. She was not entered in any race on the circuit from Florida west to California. She was not entered in the two World

Championships that took place in Key West but she did race Atlantic City. If the owner was looking to place well on the circuit skipping races made no sense. She did enter every race north of Florida. Her record of finishes was less than respectable.

Angus and the detective looked carefully at the boat pictures. Most racers in motorsports live by sponsorship money. Majestic had the usual stickers for gas, motor oil, engine manufacturer and anything else that would have earned them sponsorship money. That looked authentic. But she didn't have a major sponsor. O.K., so a guy from Staten Island purchases a $500,000 world class race boat that he keeps in Florida. He doesn't care where he places in the points or if he wins. He doesn't ride in the boat himself, apparently doesn't need the money and hasn't even bothered to paint the boat a different color than Falcone's original Seahawk blue. He's not in it for ego or for money, or for making the racing scene, so what's he in it for?

The intel on Tony was pretty much what they expected. He was from Newark's North Ward. He had owned a pizza place in Newark before the riots pushed him to Long Branch where he had owned another joint before moving to Shoretown. O.K, he wasn't just off the boat.

Law enforcement had been aware of food joints and organized crime for years. There has to be a way to launder dirty money through cash businesses. Angus told the detective about stumbling upon the wireless phone calls to and from Farquar. He asked if he knew a lawyer named Karl Pederson. The detective knew him of course, the divorce schlock who spent a lot of time hanging out at The Bar. He told Angus that there were a lot of rumors about the guy being a sleaze, and that he was really well off with a house on Barnegat Bay. Angus told him about the two conversations he had heard during which the only thing they talked about was that one had ordered a pizza for the other. They decided that the detective would check further into Pederson and Angus would listen to the tapes of Farquar's phone calls every day. They were both convinced they were on it but they needed more. They had another beer and left.

Angus knew there was too much here. He had a bunch of players from North Jersey and a pizza joint, a race boat from Miami that didn't do a whole lot of racing and totally bogus phone conversations originating with the guy who set him up. The detective got back to him 3 days later with word that Pederson was from the Newark area as well and that his father had been a well regarded criminal defense lawyer who had represented some low level "made" guys while sonny boy was a law clerk. Four days later Angus got the call he was waiting for when Farquar and Pederson were at it on the phone again. Angus met his detective friend and played him the tape. The detective took Angus directly to the County Prosecutor and they put it all in front of him. That night Angus was in the prosecutor's unmarked parked across the side street from Tony's place watching the back alley. Another unmarked was down the block from Farquar's and Pederson was receiving similar treatment. The Shoretown P.D. was not informed of the surveillance and there was a cover story in place in case Farquar suspected anything.

That night nothing happened. They listened to the tape again. Pederson was clearly telling Farquar that he was having a pizza delivered to him that night, 10pm to be exact. They staked the three places out again the following night. 10pm passed. At 11pm a box truck marked as a produce company from Newark pulled behind the store. The message had been clear code for "the drop is one day and one hour later then I am telling you." They watched the doors swing open over the loading dock and lost sight of what was coming out or going in. Ten minutes later the truck exited the alley and turned west toward the Garden State Parkway with the unmarked Angus was in following. The truck didn't turn north onto the Parkway toward Newark as they expected. It turned south. They followed it to Forked River where it turned east, crossed Route 9 and rolled into a small marina on a creek off the bay. That's when they saw her, and Angus felt the jolt through his body. The box truck for Majestic was sticking out of a shed with no doors. The box truck with that beautiful, huge picture of that beautiful blue race boat attached to that beautiful boat itself. They drove right by the marina and went around a curve before they turned back, lights off and parked off the road a discreet distance away. They waited until the two guys who had been in the truck left the marina in a car with Florida plates before they turned the unmarked around and left. They called it in and were told nothing had been seen by the surveillance at either Farquar's or Pederson's.

The Prosecutor made a call to a judge, got him out of bed, and had a search warrant issued before 2am. The unmarked covering Farquar's took the place of the unmarked that followed the delivery truck south. By 4am all three cars were staking out Tony's joint and they waited with a search warrant knowing that nothing had left the store.

Angelo showed up at 5am and unlocked the door. Hell of a time to start making pizza. He didn't step inside before he was on the sidewalk in handcuffs. Nothing was out of order until they opened a freezer that was at least 4 times the size of what you would expect from a store front pizza place. Inside were so many boxes marked "produce" that Angelo would have had to own a dozen places to use that much stuff. They opened the first one and found tomatoes. Ditto for numbers 2,3,4,5, and six. They moved the front row and hit pay dirt. Each box opened contained the plastic bags they expected to find. Some were labeled "flour" and some were labeled "baking soda". One detective broke out the small test kit each of the unmarked cars carried. He made a small incision in a bag, placed a small amount of the white powder in the bag that came with the test kit and broke the capsule containing the chemical that turned the cocaine blue. Angelo made the trip from his store to the Prosecutor's office and was singing before he even got out of the car. They nailed Farquar at his home before he got up at 6am. Apparently he slept in the nude because he was wearing one of those wrap around velcro towels when they half carried him to the car. The story that left the Prosecutor's office had him crying like a baby and holding on to his wife before they let him put on the towel and dragged him away. He sang by 7:00. At 8:30 a car left the Prosecutor's Office for Pederson's home on the Bay. Another headed for his law office.

Karl Pederson was enjoying his morning coffee sitting on his big deck behind his big house next to his big pool with the big built in soaking tub. He admired the Fountain 33 foot go fast boat that he had Reggie fountain personally build for him, perched on her lift above the bulkhead. It was the only one Fountain had ever built in that color, a shimmering platinum with matching outdrives.

He had suggested to his wife that she go to the gym. Good thing for her she did. Karl was not in a hurry to go to the office. He sat and reflected on where he was in his life and he was more than pleased.

He was inside refilling his coffee when the doorbell rang. He checked his Rolex, 8:15. He looked through the peep hole on the front door to see a guy with a pizza box. He opened the door wide and motioned for the driver to follow him in and set the box on the kitchen counter.

He got out, "I didn't expect you this early", when the first .22 caliber bullet crashed through the back of his skull followed by 2 more. He hit the floor on his face. For only a second he felt as though a weight so heavy he could not move was pinning him down. The shooter put a foot under him and into his stomach and rolled him over. He was probably already dead, but to be sure, the shooter put 2 more in through his right ear. The nice thing about a .22 is how clean it is. The low velocity tiny rounds usually stay inside the skull like a pin ball inside an arcade game and do a couple of revolutions through brain matter before they stop without exiting. Karl would have been pleased his face wasn't messed up.

Five days later just after sunset Father James stood in a cemetery, made the sign of the cross and blessed the grave of Karl Pederson. He then asked God to forgive him the anger he had felt and for the act he was about to perform. Then he kept the last part of the promise he had made to himself when he confronted Karl at The Bar.

REQUIEM FOR THE MASSES

Terry Kirkman /The Association.

Father James entered his room to the ringing of the phone. He was overjoyed to hear Sylvia's voice and he couldn't wait to tell her of his chance meeting with the lawyer but she gave him no time to speak. He recognized that she would control this conversation and that it was serious.

"James, we need to talk," Oh my god she is pregnant was the first thought that raced across his mind. She anticipated his thought. "No, I am not pregnant. I am a nurse and my man is a Roman Catholic priest and I am not stupid."

All those things were true. Maybe HE was stupid. "I need you to come over now." "Can't we talk about it over the phone. At least tell me what this is about." "No, I need to look you in the eyes and you need to see into me. Please come."

Father James left his room and turned right up the hall toward the main dining room separating him from Father Gambina's quarters. There was Gambina in his office. Father James blurted out his need to be gone for the rest of the day and the evening. He heard Gambina start to say something about "This being inconvenient -----" but he missed the rest as he turned away and fled down the hall, out the door and to his car.

He was barely conscious of turning out of the church and heading for the Parkway. His replaying of their relationship was a tangle of emotions that flooded and overwhelmed with each memory. His mind took him down one path and then yanked him onto another as he searched for a clue as to why she had summoned him so urgently and the thought of driving for an hour with the thought of losing her was almost more than he could stand.

He often thought that God had sent him an angel when he lay physically battered and broken. She was young then, barely 20, but he was only a few years older. He recalled how he felt a presence about her the moment she walked into his room. It was she who took the lead. She found reasons to come to his room often. He found himself longing for her presence. Their communication deepened with each visit and they never seemed to finish their conversation before she had to move on to the next patient. He made her think and he challenged her intellect. They became more personal and mentally intimate.

Over time he found himself longing to see her move as she walked into his room. He loved the smell of her hair as she leaned over him. Her touch on an arm or a leg took on new meaning. The shared innocent physical intimacy over the weeks stirred him and took him to a place he had not been before. Before her he could fight off the impulses of a young straight man. Now he was intoxicated and it was hopeless and he even wished it would happen. It was she who made the move. She had not planned it and that made it even better the first time because it was natural and easy. She was tending to him and they were not talking when she looked into his eyes and saw who he was and what he longed for. She locked the door and came to him, giving the gift that only a loving relationship can bring. In the union of body and mind he found a state of grace he had never experienced. He remembered the joy he felt when they were lying together and she teased him, giggling about how HE had seduced her: "I was so open.

You were safe, a priest, and you seduced me and look at the mess you have gotten us into." Now he raced on, almost sick to his stomach with the thought he might lose her.

He raced through the Lincoln Tunnel barely aware of the traffic around him. He had driven this route for 18 years and it was as though the car knew where it was going while his mind flew from thought to thought. What had he said? What had he done? Had she met someone else?

He reflected over the relationship. After he left the hospital they had continued their communion of body and soul. They never talked about it. Sylvia simply gave him her apartment address and number and the relationship deepened in the privacy of her home. He loved her in a way that any man can love a woman. He was a man when he was with her and he came to understand how important the balance she provided was to him. Sometimes they didn't leave the apartment and got lost in conversation over dinner that resumed over breakfast. Other times they simply wandered along the river front or walked to Central Park. They loved to hold on to each other when the winter wind screamed through the buildings and they loved to watch the summer sun set over the river. His priest's collar had never seen the inside of her home. He came to love the 1.5 hour drive from Jersey during which he made the transition. He left his other life behind him and the closer he got the happier he became in the anticipation. Not this time.

Sylvia had come from a non-observant Jewish household. Her father had a store in the garment district on 36th Street. Her mother was a school nurse. Sylvia had wanted to be a nurse since she was little when her mother held her against her starched white uniform and told her little girl how nurses help people. Sylvia had the intellect to become anything she wanted to become and she breezed through nursing school right after high school with no thought to further her formal education.

When two minds connect and the energy begins we want more. So it was with them. James played the mentor. Sylvia found herself asking questions about his faith and his life experience. She was drawn into conversation that needed to continue after she had finished tending to him as a nurse. He took her to places out of the City, the only life she had ever known. He took her to philosophy and religion and she soaked it up. He looked forward to when they re-met and she would lead off with a question about what they discussed last. It was delicious and he could not comprehend that it would end.

He parked the car in the parking garage down the street and hurried along the sidewalk past the cart where the smell of roasting chestnuts became the smell of the city. "No chestnuts for you today?", asked the vendor with the Turkish accent who recognized James immediately in spite of his haste. James made no reply and the vendor seemed disappointed that he did not respond at least with a quick joke. That was his usual way. James entered the lobby and pushed the button on Sylvia's apartment number. Instead of the intercom coming alive with her usual greeting or her teasing him about who he was and what he wanted, the door immediately buzzed and he pushed it open. The elevator to the 6th floor took forever but it gave him time to breathe deeply and somewhat calm himself down.

She opened the door wearing a tee shirt and jeans, bare feet, with her hair pulled back and held with a band. She had not put on makeup but that could not conceal how beautiful she was. He felt crushed when she let him in and did not touch him. She immediately turned toward the island dividing the kitchen from the living area, sat on a bar stool on the far side and motioned him to the stool on the other. He tried to take her hand but she moved it away. He tried to ask her what this was about but she stopped him by gently bringing her finger to her lips. Man and Woman can be complicated and sometimes men are stupid and the woman has more wisdom. Sometimes the woman just wants to be heard because her life is more complicated than his because she is a woman. This was one of those times.

She began as she had rehearsed. When she was sure he was settled she turned and looked out over the river. "I have loved you as well as I can. I have never questioned why or whether it was right or the fact that you are a priest. I never looked beyond the day we were spending together. I have only wanted more of them. I do not know where my life would be if we had not found each other and it is not like I haven't had other opportunities. Sometimes things happen that catch us off guard and make us think."

His heart beat through his chest. "Here it comes. Who is he and for how long has she known this? I never knew and I can't believe she would ever live a lie with me."

She continued. "I never considered life without you, but I have been offered a position at John Hopkins in Baltimore."

Baltimore! He was back in the game. "That is only 2 hours from Shoretown and the drive is easy, or I can request a transfer."

"NO, it is not that simple. It made me think James. I am 38 and where are we going?"

A child! He had considered that most women want a family and he wondered if she would at some point also. "Is it about children?"

She turned and looked at him for the first time. "It's not about me James it is about YOU. You have taught me so much and we have taught each other so much and I feel equal in so many ways and now I feel that I can't go on the way things are." Damn, she started to cry and she had told herself she was strong enough not too. But the frustration that he did not see and that he might not see and that she might lose him was too much. He got up and tried to hug her, to stop the tears, but she would have none of it.

"I want more. I want it all. I want you as my husband and I want us to have children. I want to come home to a house together every day. I want to go out to dinner with friends. I want to be in a community and I want to be in church while my husband preaches and then I want to go home with him. You can not tell me that our relationship has not made you a better man and a better priest. I see it, I feel it and you know it." There, it was all out.

Thank God. She wasn't leaving. She was coming closer than he had ever dared hope for.

"I have watched you grow so much as a man and a human being and as a priest and that is because you have been with me. Your Church can not ever convince me that you loving me is wrong."

"Of course it isn't wrong, that is why I am here and will always be for you."

She felt herself getting angry and she did her best to control it as more poured out. Once she broke the dam she could not stop. "Then you should want more. You should want what I want, a normal, honest life for a man and a woman who love each other and all the enrichment that goes with it. I see your joy when we are together. I love you for it and I feast off of it. A stupid celibacy rule written by a bunch of controlling old men in eleven hundred and something demeans you and denies that God created you as a man. If "we" are not wrong to you personally, then why are "we" only "we" when you are not a priest?

You have taught me so much about spirituality that I now have to ask you this: What is the spiritual nature of a church that denies it's faithful servant happiness and makes him keep his woman hidden. The very act of denying I exist demeans YOUR spirituality. I can no longer live like your CONCUBINE. If you believed our relationship was wrong you would never have kept it going for 18 years. Eighteen years of hiding James."

"You don't understand the Church's position on marriage and why I can love you and give you all I have and still love my Church as it is."

"I have sat in another Church James while you were preaching at yours. I have gone to Church with you when we traveled. I understand it's beauty and it's peacefulness and I believe in the good that it does. But I do not understand an institution that denies the right to love another human being and to have a family."

"My marriage to the Church makes me closer to God."

"Your marriage to the Church is total hypocrisy on their part. Your Church passed a Pastoral Provision 10 years ago that allows Protestant Clergy to become priests and retain their families. Yet, you, as one of the faithful from the beginning, are denied the right. This serves the institution, not the priest or his flock."

"Yes, and this has caused problems in some parishes where they were not accepted." He cursed himself for turning this into a debate on doctrine instead of keeping it about them.

She pounced on it. "And what of the gay priests? You know who many of them are. You went to a "lavender seminary" for a year and transferred for god's sake. I know you believe that sexual orientation is not a choice and I know you would not deny anyone gay the right to love. Isn't that what life is all about James, opportunities to love? We are a burst of energy at a point of time and we found each other and I will not go on without growing what we have."

He was speechless. She had brought so many thoughts at one time that he could not defend his position as a priest, could not think of the directive or canon or provision.

She got it all out. "I love you because you are spiritual, not because you sell the Church's line. Your parish loves you because of your spiritual being, at least the ones who think. I know you believe in the "oneness" of humanity and tolerance and understanding. I have seen you open your heart to everyone without exception and that you are only prejudice when you judge the individual as good or bad based on how they treat others. Ask yourself this James: "You serve the Church but does the Church serve you?"

She told him to leave and think about all she had said. He walked to the door and turned to look at her. He saw her face as he had never seen her before. There was no joy, only anguish and she pushed him through the door into the hall before he could speak. She shut it and locked him out and she could not control herself any longer. He heard her first cry before she retreated to the bedroom. He slumped against the wall in the hallway and it held him up as he dragged himself to the elevator, down and out.

DREAMS

Roy Orbison

The pizza caper in Shoretown wasn't the first time an independently owned business was used to distribute drugs and launder dirty money. On March 2, 1987 the longest criminal jury trial in U.S. history wrapped up in federal court. The scope was international and brought down the suppliers in Switzerland and Spain and 22 defendants scattered around the New York City area. Evidence introduced showed that over 1.6 billion dollars worth of heroin was brought to the U.S. between 1975 and 1984. Rudy Giiuliani was the United States Attorney for the Southern District of New York. Although he did not try the case, his investigations were critical to obtaining the convictions. He later became Mayor of NYC.

The bust in Shoretown was the result of Angus out to clear his name. Angus probably didn't anticipate the consequences. The Mayor announced early on that he was not going to seek re-election. He was never connected to the scheme in any way, probably had just had enough. He appointed a temporary Police Chief to replace Farquar until they could have a civil service exam and name a permanent replacement. Two other cops went down with Farquar, both of whom had been with him the night he set Angus up. The Town did not offer Angus his job back. He wouldn't have taken it anyway.

The Mayor recognized Rocco Rinaldi's success, talent and popularity. He had appointed Rocco to the Municipal Utilities Authority several years before and he served as one of 5 Commissioners. The Utility was responsible to provide water and sewer services to 3 towns that were growing and putting demands on the infrastructure that the locals did not anticipate. Rocco was voted Chairman of the Board and he proceeded to put his business organization skills and knowledge of construction to good use. He demanded a balanced budget and charged the finance chairman and auditor with coming back to the Board with a 5 year financial plan. The Board met many nights to project long term capital improvements, how they were going to pay for them and what the customers water rates were going to be. Once he had the finances under control and long term infrastructure projects funded he placed the Utility on cruise control under the direction of a young, responsible and loyal employee who had worked his way up the ladder and was not connected politically.

Angus and Father James arrived at Rocco's office at about the same time, neither one knowing why Rocco wanted them to come over. After a short time Rocco got to the point.

"I have given it a lot of thought and I want to run for Mayor. If I jump in early I think I can make it. The guy in is out. The Democrats have to replace him with a new candidate and the Republicans haven't named a candidate. I want to take a run as an Independent."

"Why don't you just go to the Republicans and try for that shot, you would already have a lot of votes and a whole organization behind you." asked Angus.

"Because then I would be no different than any other office holder who owes his bones to the party. I know how the game is played. When the Mayor appointed me to the Utilities Authority the first thing he did was set up a meeting between me and our State Senator. They made it clear they thought I had potential and that if I went with them I would be groomed for office. He assumed I owed him. Yeah, I owed him. I owed him the best job I could do. I don't need their money and I lost my ego a long time ago. Politics sucks. The best and brightest don't rise to the top. They may start out that way, but if they are lifetime politicians they have made enough deals and owe enough people inside and outside to taint every decision they make. Principal gets kicked to the curb and by the time they rise to the next office they are bought and paid for. I either win as an Independent or I don't win."

"I don't know how much I can help." said Angus. Rocco knew the Prosecutor's Office had offered Angus a position as Investigator soon after the pizza caper wrapped up. The guys on the county level got Angus and Angus got his brotherhood back. Angus was seen very differently then he had been a year before. Now everybody was his friend. The employees in town hall who snubbed Sally now wanted to take her to lunch. Angus and Sally heard the same litany over and over, "We knew you weren't guilty of anything---couldn't figure out why they were out to get you----wish we had known-----," Yeah, and you were there to help us right?

"Father, I want you to be my Treasurer. Who better to handle money then a priest? Anyway, you don't need to raise money, I'll fund this myself. Do you think that Father Gambina will allow it?"

"I have shocked Father Gambina since the day I arrived years ago. I really don't care what he thinks."

"My sister Annie is organizing a woman's group to line up neighborhood coffees and support any public appearances that I need to make. I really don't think I need a campaign manager. She'll keep the calendar."

"So what happens to your business?", asked Angus.

"Did Washington give up Mount Vernon? Did Jefferson give up Monticello? Having a business to go home to is what keeps you from having to become a lifetime politician and selling out. I have a great staff and my business will run just fine. I don't need the money that public office can produce and I can act in the best interest of the people, and I don't give a damn because I don't have to get reelected to have an income. Rather liberating don't you think?"

So it was done. Annie set about getting Rocco enough signatures to get him onto the ballot and Father set up the candidate with the necessary State of New Jersey forms and Rocco funded the bank account. Rocco took a one year lease on the billboard he had his eye on for a long time. He placed the word "THINK" on the biggest, baddest, most strategically placed billboard in Shoretown. That was all, just "THINK". The newspaper had a field day with it, stretching the speculation about who had placed it there and what it meant. A month later he added, "RINALDI". "THINK RINALDI". Think Rinaldi why?????? A month after that "FOR MAYOR" was added. "THINK RINALDI FOR MAYOR" kicked off and they never looked back.

AMERICAN LAND
Bruce Springsteen

I settled into my routine of living Key West. Working the boat business gave me a lot of energy and the truth is, I didn't miss racing. I had thought that I would go hang out at the first race of the year at Marathon only a few miles away. But as the day grew closer I found myself rethinking it. Did I really want to watch my friends roaring off while I stayed on the beach? Did I really want the whole party scene? I had already turned down a bunch of offers to throttle. All the way in or all the way out. Don't look back you can never go back. I didn't go.

So why was I restless? There was so much positive going on in my life why couldn't I just enjoy it? Business was great and Floyd appreciated it. He put me on profit sharing and I was making 4 times what I had made as a teacher. I bought a house on Seminary Street, north of Duval. It didn't have the pedigree that Floyd and Kate's did but it was fine for me. It was a typical Florida new construction, cinder block with a concrete stucco finish in an off white. The lot had a mature banyon tree on it and I planted bird of paradise, crotons and thai. Stick a twig in the ground in Florida during the rainy months and it grows. My yard looked great. I had sunk my roots. Land in Key West was at a premium but I had enough driveway to park 2 cars and a back yard big enough for a hot tub and tiki bar.

The Wenches were still glad to see me. The bar tenders at the Green Parrot were still glad to see me. The boat builders and marina staff treated me like a brother. Floyd and Kate treated me like family and we were about to make it official. Kate was due in 4 months and they had already asked me to be the Godfather. I prayed the kid was going to be a boy. I had no idea what to do with a little girl other than to never leave her side until I got the word from Kate that it was o.k. to turn her loose. I was already planning the make and model of the shotgun I would use if any of the high school boys tried anything on my watch.

I was in the hot tub alone, reflecting on all these things, enjoying a cigar and rum straight up with a lime, when the phone rang. The phone was strategically placed within reach so I answered it:

"Hi, this is Angus Davitt."

"Angus Davitt from the bridge? Son of a bitch, how did you find my home phone?"

"Not hard since I am an investigator with the County Prosecutor's Office."
"You're here in Key West?"

"No, I am freezing my ass off in New Jersey. Thought you might like to hear about what happened after I met you on the bridge that night."

Angus told me all about how he had recognized the blue cat Majestic the moment he saw it in the race program and how it had taken him back to that night in Shoretown. I thought he had retired from the department, not gotten thrown off. He went on to tell me about who went down when they busted the players. When he got to Karl Pederson being hit I choked on my rum. That was the first I heard of him since 1970. A lot can happen to a man in 20 years.

"I've got a few more surprises for you. Can I come down and talk to you?"

"Of course, come on down and warm up."

MARGARITAVILLE
Jimmy Buffett

Basic business: Find a demand and fill it. No one held a silver spoon with white powder up to the nose of the American public and forced them to snort it. No one shoved a joint into the American mouth, lit it, and forced the public to inhale. The American public loved weed and loved cocaine and both went great with good alcohol. Everyone made nice nice getting high. South American drug cartels didn't create the demand, they filled it.

I personally had no use for cocaine. A decent joint of unadulterated mellow weed was sweet. The desire for anything above that was lost on me. I had lived through the innocent days when half of the residents of Key West were either smoking weed or arranging inventive ways to profit from it. Cocaine brought nasty. Big business breeds big profits. Big profits need to be protected. Just like prohibition created criminals, so did the illegal drug trafficking. I am sure that most consumers sticking shit up their noses didn't think about what it took to get it to them.

So, you have this illegal product in South and Central America in great demand in the U.S. How do you get it here? The Straits of Florida have been the major trade route for water travel since about 1492. The Spanish enslaved the Mexicans, Central and South Americans, plundered their gold and silver and shipped it all back on treasure ships. The first stop from Central America and Mexico was Havana, Cuba. There the ships were consolidated, loaded and sailed up the coast of the Florida Keys riding the Gulf Stream north.

Fast forward to 1980 or so. Pot required large containers. Cargo ships of all varieties were employed, and just like Prohibition, the business model of transferring the product to small boats for the final leg into port worked fine. If you were going to smuggle by air, the plane of choice was the DC 3 twin engine work horse of WWII vintage. Smaller aircraft were employed and abandoned where they landed all over Florida.

Cocaine was much more profitable. A light aircraft might be able to carry 4 million dollar street value worth of cocaine on one trip. A go fast boat could carry much more, perhaps 70 million. Technology drives industry profits. The Feds cooperated with the Colombian government and law enforcement intensified efforts to stem the tide. Air smuggling became a logistical problem when the U.S. Air Force began to use "Aerostats", or tethered radar system balloons. The balloons were secured by 25,000 feet of cable and could stay aloft until the winds reached 65 mph, which meant they were aloft most of the time. The very first was on Cudjoe Key overlooking the Straits of Florida. It provided low level radar coverage with a range of 200 miles. That range was way beyond any possible route a cocaine laden airplane coming up from the South could have flown at low altitude to enter the U.S.

Cudjoe Key is located at mile marker 21. That is also charted as 24.696119 North, 81.504511 West, in universal navigational terms. Navigators have always used the stars and sun to find out where they are at any time at any place on earth. In 1851 Greenwich, England became the first really scientific attempt to develop "longitude" and the Greenwich Meridian serves as "0" degrees.

Basically, "Latitude" measures where you are horizontally on the earth based on rings equal distant from the Equator. "Longitude" measures where you are vertically. Determining this required "shooting the sun" with a sextant, a very accurate time piece, and locating where you are on a printed map. Navigator's relied on a number of devices to determine position based on how far you have traveled in a given direction. I grew up running a boat with a watch, tachometer and compass which allowed me to approximate where I was in order to get back to where I came from. This "dead reckoning" was very useful in fog or a storm when you couldn't see past the windshield and there was no GPS.

In 1960 Dr. Iven Getting, a graduate of M.I.T. and a Graduate Rhode's Scholar, worked with the Raytheon Corporation to create a satellite grid for the U.S. Department of Defense known as "Global Positioning System." Eventually "GPS" became 18 satellites on 3 orbital planes read by devices that can tell you within feet where you are anywhere on earth. In 1983 President Reagan freed the system up for civilian use. Have a cell phone? You have a GPS.

GPS revolutionized smuggling. This was a very useful technology. Now you knew in feet how close you were to a rendezvous. Or, you could leave a drop for someone to pick up later and know exactly where it was. The devices were cruder and not as common as those in use today, but they worked. That was a beautiful thing for smuggling because flying the shit in became more difficult thanks to the radar technology employed by our government. Another rule of business, adapt or perish.

The solution to avoid detection was to fly the stuff into the Bahamas and put it onto fast boats that made the short trip to the east coast of Florida. That took the radar in the Keys out of play. Then the Feds found out about the Falcone's and Magluda's of the world and it became problematic to run in from the Bahamas. Surface boats were becoming more and more vulnerable as the Feds fought fire with fire and employed aircraft to spot smugglers and go fast boats to catch them. The smugglers used technology to stay one step ahead.

The first attempts at smuggling drugs up from South and Central America in submerged, or partially submerged vessels, was fairly sophisticated for the early 90's, but nothing like today when the cartels are building multi-million dollar, fully functional submarines. In 1989 drug enforcement found an empty 21 foot cylinder designed to be towed floating off Boca Raton, FL. The Coast Guard dubbed it "Big Foot" because they had heard about it but hadn't seen it. It had a hatch that could only be opened from the outside. Ballast tanks allowed it to be programmed to ride along 30 feet under water and it had a buoy with a GPS transmitter in case whatever was towing it needed to cut it loose. It could carry, what at that time, was cocaine with a wholesale value of 70 million dollars. This was a brilliant use of business technology.

When Angus hung up from our phone call I drained the rum and burned the cigar down to my lips concentrating on speculating about why he, law enforcement, had called me. Why was I so special that a casual acquaintance a thousand miles away called me on business? I settled on perhaps they wanted our company to build boats for the DEA. Geeze was I wrong.

Angus had called me at 4pm. My doorbell rang at 10pm. I remembered what Angus looked like from our brief meeting that night on the bridge. Angus cleaned up pretty good and the guy he was with wore a tie and looked like an accountant. I ushered them in and headed for the tiki bar in the back. "You guys up for a margarita?"

Angus answered, "Yeah, but lets have it inside where we can talk."

Right, who needs the neighbors hearing what's going on. I am talking to a cop and I don't know who the other guy is. Start thinking like a cop. How do I do that?

We settled into the living room and Angus got right to the point.

"I know you want to know about Pederson. I've got a few other surprises for you. Remember Father James and Rocco from West Orange?"

I spent the next few minutes with my mouth hanging open as Angus told me how he had returned to Shoretown and, after putting the pizza caper together told them both about the guy he met on the bridge who got the whole thing started. I asked him for their phone numbers.
"Of course, but not yet. I didn't come all the way to Florida to tell you this. I came to Florida because you need to do something for us. Here is my badge and ID. I don't want you thinking this is some kind of crazy deal."

"Who is "us" and who is this? You haven't introduced him."

"This would be federal agent Caulfield."

"And what agency is federal agent Caulfield from?" I didn't like where this was going.

"Just know he is federal and heading up a special task force. We're here to tell you all you need to know and not what you don't need to know." Stone Face said nothing.

The first act of their little drama had been to catch me up to date on what went on in Shoretown, why Pederson was killed and who they thought did it. They told me they had followed the ladder up until they identified the guy in Long Island who owned Majestic, but they couldn't connect him to anything. He claimed the boat was stolen and he didn't know it was gone. They went to the riding crew who raced it, but they were hired guns from California who flew in before each race and left afterward. That took the investigation to the boat yard where the boat was kept in Florida.

"A week ago we got lucky. Most of our drug busts happen because of an informant. We usually don't want the informant, we want to go as high up the food chain as we can. In this case we believe the informant is not involved. We do know she is scared shitless and has been trying to get out of a relationship with the bad guy for a couple of years. We can get her out and we can get a lot higher in this organization, but we need your help. "Mute Stone Face, sitting next to Angus, finally had something to say, "The informant is Jessie, your ex-wife. We need one more player to make this happen and we want it to be you."

If they had planned for Stone Face to drop the bomb on me for affect it had worked. I had one of those moments where my mind shuts everything off but what it needs to make sense of, attacking this from all angles at the same time like lightning flying around lighting things up. The emotion of hearing Jessie's name caught me off guard and I had no time to do anything but react mentally. It all came togther and I knew in a second that I cared more about her now than I had cared before.

Angus jumped back in. "Let me tell you that Jessie's o.k, for now, how I got involved, and why we are here. After the bust in Shoretown the Prosecutor's Office offered me a job as investigator. They figured I was a great fit for narcotics. Our informant in Jersey is a low level guy, really just a user. But he could tell us when a new shipment had arrived. We had heard that a single engine Cessna was using the unfinished interstate out past Wall Township for touch and go landings. We put two and two together and were there to bust the pilot and the dealers doing the pick up. We traced the plane's numbers back to Marathon Airport in the Keys. We had two forms of delivery to Jersey; one the race boat I busted, and two the Cessna. So my office sends me down to be a part of Mr. Caulfield's task force. Caulfield's office runs down the marina lead.

We found it was owned by a guy by the name of Ray who owned a dive shop in Key Largo during the 70's and 80's. All we can find is that he runs, what appears to be a clean operation. But, for a guy who owns a small marina in Homestead, Florida he sure has a nice house in Miami. Paid cash for it. Paid cash for the marina too. Want to set me up with another drink?"

Angus was good, great sense of timing. Give me time to think and let it all sink in. I left them sitting on the couch and walked to the tiki bar to mix the drinks. My thoughts went to Jessie. I had spent the past 4 years since I saw her in Ray's dive shop trying to forget her. Angus played it perfectly.

"Jessie knew Ray was doing some kind of crap because of their lifestyle, but she didn't know what. She told us that at first it was alright because she assumed he took the money from the sale of the dive shop and put it into the marina. She is not a stupid girl, never saw the books, but knew what the property looked like and that there was no way it could generate the money he had. He kept her out of it. She told us the only time he ever laid a hand on her was when she asked him about this a couple of years ago. When she pushed it he cracked her in the face and told her to shut up, that he had given her this lifestyle and it was his business, not hers and she was his too and that she wasn't going anywhere."
Angus answered my question before I asked it. "She never married the guy and she's stuck as the girlfriend and sees no way out."

"We know all this because she got home from the gym earlier than expected a week ago and walked into a situation. She was surprised to see Ray had a guest. He was out by the pool with Billy, a kid she had taught in high school in Key Largo 6 years before. She knew him to be the son of a charter boat captain, at that time more interested in partying than learning his father's business or going to college. She saw them but they didn't see her. The doors were open and she caught enough of the conversation about another shipment arriving to put it all together. She left without

Ray knowing she had been there to begin with. Smart girl. She called the county Sheriff's office from the bar where she was trying to steady her nerves. They put her in touch with Mr. Caulfield. He had her drive into Lauderdale, far enough away from Ray, where his agents collected her. She told them all she knew and we had Billy bagged the next morning in Key Largo. He rolled over and now he's the informant. Mr. Caulfield told him they had tailed him from Key Largo to cover Jessie. This isn't the first time Billy worked for Ray. He spills it all and Mr. Caulfield finds out Billy is doing the transport from offshore into the coast."

"They call me in for a briefing on the whole situation. They show me a picture of Jessie, this her?"

They didn't have to ask me if it was. The years had treated her well, except that she wore an expression I had never seen on her.

"I know that this is going fast, but here is the bottom line", says Caulfield.

Duh, no shit it's all going fast and the only reason I am still listening is because of Jessie but you already knew that. I thought it but I didn't say it.

"There is another delivery coming in. We contacted Jessie and told her to hang in there for another couple of days and we would put her in a safe house the night it goes down, three days from now. We assured her when we made the bust it would be all over for her. We told her that Billy was making another pick up and that we were going to put someone with him who could handle the boat. We couldn't afford to have Billy make a mistake and jeopardize what was going down. When we told her we needed to put someone in the boat with Billy she never hesitated and said she wanted it to be you. You two ran boats together a lot of years. She told us that she knew you were racing. Ray had taken her down to the Worlds in Key West and she watched you but you never knew it. No way Ray was going to let her be around you."

Angus got back in. "When I heard your name it was a 'holy crap' moment for me. Then we talked it over and thought you were perfect. You have the experience to get it done. You also have the perfect cover, just another offshore racer looking to make a quick buck.

"Yeah, and don't forget I still care about the woman."

"Bingo"!

"This is what Billy lays on us: Last week a shipment of cocaine worth 70 million wholesale left Columbia by boat and Ray is the receiving party. Billy is supposed to do what he has done in the past, pick it up somewhere out in the Gulf Stream and take it to a land location. He doesn't know what boat he is using, he doesn't know where it is berthed, he doesn't know where the pick up point is in the Gulf Stream and he doesn't know where he is taking it. In the past, when the deal was done and he put the boat where he was supposed to, he walked away from the boat and rode away on the motorcycle provided for him. He never saw who off loaded the stuff. These guys are careful."

"Three nights from now Billy will go to the gas station at the corner of U.S. 1 and Reef Drive at the entrance to Key Largo. The pay phone will ring and he will be told where the boat is and how to identify it. He tells us that there will be a pager on the driver's seat and that the message will be the numbers of the GPS coordinates for the transfer. He never comes back to the place where he picked the boat up and he won't know where to drop it until they give him the coordinates at sea when the go-fast is loaded. We made sure the guy he usually takes with him has met with an unfortunate circumstance and is being held in the county jail for a few days. We are taking precautions to make sure Ray doesn't know. If he does find out, Billy knows what to say to cover. You are a great fit with Billy because he will remember you from when you were a teacher and married to Jessie. He is young, stupid and scared, but the one thing that rang true is that he doesn't want to see Jessie get hurt. Still want to ask what your role is going to be?"
"Terrific. You want me to take a boat I have never seen before, with a guy who's a putz, to meet up with Colombian drug smugglers, somewhere, we don't know where, between here and the Bahamas, and bring the shipment back to, we don't know where. I might get shot by the Colombians, or the Bahama's military, or the Coast Guard or Customs or Mr. Caulfield's agency, whatever that is, or a local cop who stumbles onto the situation or maybe Ray is being extra careful on this one or maybe Billy tipped him off or maybe Jessie can't be an actress long enough. And, since you have no idea where we are going, how are you going to protect us and nail them?"

Caulfield's turn, "We don't know exactly where you are going, but we do know you are coming into the east coast of Florida or the upper Keys. We will give you a GPS transponder that we can read from 20 miles away. Believe me I have the resources to be where we need to be when you flip it on and we follow you."

"So why don't you go get Joe Blow to run the boat? Oh wait a minute. I have to do it because Jessie asked for me and you know that as long as I am doing it for her you can trust me too and that if I run the boat you have the best chance of making the whole thing work. When do I meet up with Billy?"

"6pm three nights from now at the gas station. You drive him to the boat and he rides."

"Screw that. He rides a bike and I ride my bike and I don't get in a car with him."

"O.K., let's work out the rest of the details," says Stone Face who smiled for the first time.

THE CHASE

Jan Hammer / Miami Vice

So here is how it went down: Three days later I arrived at the gas station at 1800. I had been informed we are on military time. I was riding my 250cc bike and I see Billy sitting on a chopper next to the phone booth. Looks just like his picture. What does one take to a smuggling operation? Caulfield gave me the GPS transponder I am not to turn on until we get within 20 miles of the coast on the return trip and a cellphone that I am not to call out on. I also had the Colt Combat Commander that got me through the Newark riots and has lived with me for years. I have a Florida concealed carry permit and I figure it's no big deal if I get stopped by law enforcement for any reason. Caulfield never said anything about a firearm so I took care of that part of the equation. I also had the divers knife that went with me anytime I was on a boat and a pocket compass. I also folded up two charts of the Florida coast. Electronics are wonderful when they work. I managed to get these items into loose fitting cargo pants with an extra long tee shirt that I covered with a down vest and nylon rain gear top. My well used driving gloves, needed on the bike and the boat, completed my concept of the well dressed smuggler. The weather forecast was for night time temps in the 60's. The marine forecast called for a 2-4 foot chop in Biscayne Bay and the same conditions in the Gulf Stream 20 miles off shore. Winds were to be light. Yeah, and this was the Gulf Stream and all bets were off.

The phone rang, Billy answered it, grunted into it a few times and announced to me that we were going to Bahia Mar Marina in Ft. Lauderdale, berth 79. We saddled up and I followed him onto the causeway to the mainland, up the Florida Turnpike and into Ft. Lauderdale. We made slip 79 just as the sun was setting and I took a good look at "Daddy's Doll", a nicely done up dark blue 46 foot Cigarette Rough Rider that I thought I recognized as one of Cigarette's factory racing hulls. The outdrives were bulletproof #6's. I looked for the hoses that pumped air into the props to get an overloaded boat up on plane but there weren't any. This was a pleasure boat, no longer a race boat. The cockpit was standard, two bolster seats forward with dual controls so I could operate the wheel and throttles at the same time with a bench seat aft and a padded deck over the engine compartment. She had registration numbers on the bow, probably fictitious, and her name ran a third of the way down her sides in script that was a blue also and got lost if you weren't looking at it straight on. Ray had thoughtfully equipped her with a radar arch over the cockpit with a radar disc and a whip VHF antennae. To all appearances this was another rich boy toy out to enjoy the lights of Miami. Given that the feds didn't want us caught I saw no reason why we would attract any attention. They assumed Billy knew who I was, but even if he didn't they wanted him to know I was in charge. They told him some story about me working as a fed while I was on the racing circuit. He never asked and I never offered.

I touched the switch that opened the engine hatch and as it rose it revealed the space below was taken up by two nice looking big blocks, 1200 HP Cobras, staggered with one in front of the other. The other thing that caught my eyes was the 2 oversize hatches on the front flat deck of the boat. I unscrewed the latches dogging down the hinged door on the bulkhead separating our cockpit from the huge forward cabin area and took a look. Aside from the construction bulkheads she was empty. Yep a dedicated race boat hull. I approved. She should do 110 mph or better empty. Could she pick herself up and run with 6,000 lbs of coke? We will see.

Billy jumped into the cockpit and no more than picked up the pager when it went off. It was obvious we were being watched by whomever set up the boat. Billy read off the numbers and I programmed them into the GPS. I fired up the Cobras and they purred. Gauges looked good and fuel was showing "full". I told Billy to cast off the lines and have a seat, I would steer and throttle. I idled her down the Stanahan River, pushed up the throttles and we soared into the Straights of Florida with the sun setting behind us.

It was one of those rare nights on the water. It was clear with almost no breeze and the new moon had not yet shown itself. Sky met water somewhere on the horizon and all was dark and calm. There was no leaping and pounding. The big boat simply put her nose up and slid forward doing a comfortable 60 mph. I let her lope along and took in the sights of the small boat fleet just off Lauderdale in close to shore. Radar had them all and I watched the blips on the screen thin out quickly as we ran straight and fast. The course took us out into the Stream and on a heading that put us 20 miles off Miami as we blew by headed for the point of a triangle made by The Bahamas, Cuba and the Keys. 60 miles out we cleared a cruise ship I had been watching on radar for a while, headed on a course for Government Cut. There were only a few radar contacts, probably fishing boats, and I swung the wheel to stay well clear of each one. The stars, never visible when you are around the lights of civilization, appeared and were brilliant and 3 dimensional against a coal black sky. I loved it.

Twenty miles from the rendezvous point I picked up a small radar blip. Nothing around it and in the middle of nowhere. I steered straight in. Pulling back the throttles as it came into view I planned a slow circle keeping a hundred yards out. I came in on the bow and saw it was a sport fisherman maybe 27 feet long with two big outboards. Small to be out here, but no big deal on a night like this. She had a full cabin forward and a flying bridge and was rigged with outriggers and everything to make her a legitimate fishing boat. I came around her port side and saw 4 figures in the cockpit illuminated by red light. Red light does not affect night vision and I knew whoever these guys were, they were boatmen. As I cleared the transom and started around the starboard side the long black cylinder came into view, tied to the side of their boat. It was shorter, maybe 20 feet long and looked like nothing more than a boiler half submerged, except there was a guy standing on it who soon disappeared through a hatch.

I continued around the stern and completed the circle coming up alongside the cylinder this time. The crew of the fishing boat was ready with lines and they threw them over the cylinder for us to secure next to it. I had Billy go forward with 4 bumpers and secure them between us and them using the center cleat on Doll's deck. Before I got the boat stopped one guy with a captain's hat motioned Billy into the cockpit of the fishing boat and handed Billy an envelope. He said something in Spanish and Billy nodded. I didn't need to know what they said. They were already swarming the cylinder that was the mule and the guy below was throwing clear, heavy plastic bags onto the deck. I could just make out the individual packs inside each one. Billy popped the hatches on Doll and the crew of the fishing boat got a line going handing each bag out of the mule into the Doll. How long does it take 4 guys to transfer 6,000lbs of individually packaged coke from boat to boat? Not long. They were going like hell and Billy came back to me with the envelope.

"What did he say," I asked. "Beats the hell out of me," answered Billy. I opened it.

"Entrance to Jewfish Creek, Boston Whaler Montauk is your friend." was all it read.

It was all I needed to know. Son of a bitch. We were going to return to the water way that cut under the bridge at the entrance to Key Largo about a mile from the phone booth where Billy got the call! To get there I would take us through the southern end of Key Biscayne and into Card Sound. Pulling out my chart, I determined to come in to shore on Palmetto Bay and run the coast down Biscayne Bay to Card Sound in order to avoid the danger of having to cut through the barrier island wildlife refuge at night. By now it was midnight and the off loading was still going on. The plan looked good and then things began to change.

Doll was getting awfully full. The guy standing in her belly was now visible from the waist up and was barely bending to deposit the bags. That's when the guy who had talked to Billy, who never left the fishing boat, said something to the 4 guys doing the off loading and the bags started going the other way into the fishing boat. I only counted 6 bags in the cockpit when his gun came out. He never looked at us. He was yelling at the crew and motioning them forward on the cylinder which was now riding high in the water, relieved of the weight. The gun looked like a twelve gauge pump shotgun to me. I eased the Colt automatic out of my cargo pants pocket and kept my hand on it under the dash board. Nobody told me I might be trading shots with a guy with a twelve gauge.

When he had them grouped forward he turned to us, his gun still on his crew. He was yelling in Spanish and I caught enough to know he wanted us to leave and leave fast. Billy was paralyzed. I got him moving.

"Get up there and untie us for Christ's sake. Can't you see he wants us gone?"

Billy got it and made his way from the cockpit to the middle cleat halfway to our bow and the line that secured us to the mule while I untied the stern line.

The captain's attention was on the crew huddled together on the front of the mule and I began to feel a sense of relief. The engines fired up instantly and I eased the port engine into gear and steered us away, going around the mule and sport fisher's bow so that the captain couldn't get a clean shot at us if he changed his mind. As we cleared the bow and headed away we had our stern to him and a clear view as he pumped rounds into the 4 poor bastards. It was clear he planned to take a small percentage of the load and he wasn't sharing. Was that the deal he had made to tow the shit to us or was he skimming off the top? Who knows. I put the automatic back into my cargo pants.

All boats are "displacement", meaning they are submerged in the water to some extent, until they skim over the top at which point they become "planing" hulls. It takes a lot of power to get a deep vee up on top and planing. That is the price you pay for a go fast boat that can run in heavy seas. If she's overloaded and you hammer the throttles she sticks her nose up in the air like a classy chick who says, "I only go as fast as I want to go." Daddy's Doll had a lot of class. Her bow was way the hell up in the air and she wouldn't step up on top. She pushed the water and couldn't or wouldn't lift her stern. The engines labored and torqued but I couldn't spin the props fast enough to get her up. The weight she was asked to carry made this a borderline situation at best. Returning to shore at 8 miles an hour, which was as fast as she would go off plane, was not an option. It was either get her up or start throwing off bundles until she was light enough.

I told Billy to get all the way forward on the deck and straddle the bow like he was a nose cone. He just looked at me scared shitless but then did what I told him. I had looked for the hoses attached to the out drives that would put air into the water around the props to help them get us up. I knew she didn't have them and it had worried me from the start. I would have to get air into the props another way. Putting air into the water around the props makes them "cavitate" or spin faster. As the boat rises the air stops, the props grab and you are planing. When Billy had all his weight forward I hammered the engines again and spun the wheel from side to side making the props suck air in from the sides of the stern. She labored, staggered and swerved like a drunk after a night on the town. I sweated and I assumed Billy was finding God. The props revved up this time and then grabbed, sending her over the top of the wave she was pushing, getting her up onto plane, and propelling us into who knew what.

An hour and a half later we saw the bright lights of Miami to our North and the lesser lights of Palmetto Bay to our South just like I had planned. Billy flipped on the transmitter so that our handlers could track us. I throttled Doll back to 40mph trying to give them time to get close. I swung us South and stayed maybe 5 miles off the coast until we picked up the point of the wildlife refuge and the entrance of Card Sound on radar. We had burned off probably 500lbs of fuel, but I didn't know if she would get back up on plane again if I throttled back too far before we had to. I eased back until the speedometer told us we were doing 35 mph and she was still on top. It took us a good half hour to make the entrance to Jewfish Creek. When we picked up the channel markers of the narrow, protected creek is when Billy spotted a small boat going like hell coming at us from the port side. When it got closer I could see it was a 17 foot Montauk, easy to spot because of her hull shape and center console. She could stay with us at this speed and she came up our side and we could see there was only one guy. He motioned for us to follow him and he broke off our course and led us toward the mangroves before we got to the Card Sound Bridge. He slowed to a crawl, we did too and he came along side.

"Out of the boat, you take this one. Take it into Lake Surprise and leave it. Your bikes are at the gas station.", was all he said.

Gladly thank you. It had been an interesting night.

We left the Montauk on the shore and walked parallel to Route 1 the short distance to the gas station. Billy and I saddled up. For the first time he told me he was going home where he would remain until the feds came and got him. He didn't seem like a bad kid, he had done well tonight and I hoped he would be all right.

I turned the bike toward the mainland riding Route 1 to avoid Card Sound. I got as far as the Last Chance Saloon when an unmarked peeled out of the parking lot and pulled me over. Two suits dragged me off the bike and cuffed me against the car in the still dark night. They threw me into the back seat and one guy climbed in with me. As we took off for the Florida Turnpike he grinned like the Cheshire Cat, pushed me forward and took off the cuffs.

"Anything you want?" he asked.

"You know what I want."
He asked me what had gone on and I gave him every detail I could, back tracking from where we dropped the Montauk so they would have the trail where last I saw it. He assured me the GPS transponder was working fine and Doll had stopped in the mangroves somewhere off of the Card Sound Road.

He handed me a bottle of water and a sandwich, shorts and a clean tee shirt and sandals. I changed in the back of the car. When I transferred the automatic to the shorts he looked but didn't say a word. The driver didn't waste anytime covering the road to Miami. They pulled up at the hotel the guy with me had told me about and he walked me to the third floor. He knocked on the door of 309 and I saw the peephole go dark from the inside for a second. The door opened with the chain still in place, then closed and opened again. The woman who opened the door was wearing a white blouse and dark pants. I saw the butt of a Detective Special sticking out of the waist band on her right side. "We got him," she said. I entered and there was Jessie running at me. I wrapped her up and the years left with our tears.

THE LONG WAY HOME

Rosanne Cash

Mayor Rocco Rinaldi's home was strategically placed on the highest piece of ground overlooking the river in Shoretown. His vista seemed endless. This was his playground for his Renee and the twins and for his oldest and dearest friends. Rocco's home office contained none of the work of his construction company. He wanted a clear separation between his profession and his service as Mayor. He lugged around no files. His desks at his home, his business and in the Mayor's office were starkly bare. He set the direction and left the day-to-day to his people. The employees of his company were fierce in their loyalty to him and the permanent staff in town hall soon felt the same way. He had no political aspirations beyond Shoretown.

The most commanding feature was the solarium, 4,000 square feet under glass, where even in the dismal Jersey winter, there was a sense of serene openness and light. This day there was special. Renee had decorated with what seemed a truckload of vibrant plants and nature cooperated with bright sun that warmed the natural stone floor and danced off the glass.

Angus and Sally picked us up at the hotel where Jessie and I had stayed for the past 2 days. I had booked the hotel before we drove up from the Keys knowing Rocco would want us to stay with him. After a separation of 20 years I wanted to keep each meeting over the couple of days we were here fresh and new and unstrained. Rocco, Father James and I spent hours re-bonding as only boyhood friends lost and now found can. Jessie gave me her blessing to leave her with Renee and that she would not be lost or overwhelmed with these old friends of mine who were strangers to her. It had only been a couple of months since she was free from Ray and out of that situation clean. I felt like I was conscious of every word that came out of my mouth and what she thought and how she felt and I was still sorting out how much was her gratitude to me for getting her out of there. I weighed those things against what emotions we had resurrected from another time and place and whether I could make them last.

When we arrived Renee pinned a carnation on my lapel and a corsage on Jessie.

The Episcopal priest, Father John, and his wife arrived 5 minutes before the ceremony was to start. Rocco had positioned a table with two white candles bordering a plain brass cross and draped with a garland of green pine bows and roses. We stood waiting for the brief ceremony that would take place a mile south of the hospital where Sylvia had taken the job of Nursing Supervisor. The Episcopal church where Father James was soon to be appointed assistant pastor was right around the corner.

Father James and Sylvia emerged from the home into the solarium and their entrance music was the applause of their friends. They walked straight across to the table where the ceremony was to take place and where the Priest and Mayor were standing. Rocco addressed them both directly.

"This has been a long journey for you both. This is a day of celebration not just witnessed, but experienced by those closest to you. The vows will be given by Father John and I will, in my official capacity as Mayor, pronounce you man and wife."

Rocco hammed up the "Mayor" bit and got the reaction he wanted. The atmosphere was festive and beautiful and unconventional and full of positive emotions and unspoken appreciation for where we had been and what it took to get here and of new beginnings.

I slid my hand into Jessie's and she leaned into me.

Father John of the Episcopal church took over. "Before beginning the ceremony we will have a reading from Calvin."

"When Father James and Sylvia asked me to read at their wedding I was at once honored and terrified. How can I know the words they will find special? How can I make this as unique as they are? First, I would remind you what Robert J. Sternberg said and apply it to marriage: 'Passion is the quickest to develop and the quickest to fade. Intimacy develops more slowly and commitment more gradually still.' James and Sylvia, you have traveled to this point in time."

"I then thought about what Father John would say during the Christian religious part of the ceremony that I know Father James and Sylvia hold so dear. Certain that their religious beliefs would be addressed I pondered the spiritual. Not all who are religious are spiritual. And if one is not spiritual can one be truly religious?"

"I am convinced that James and Sylvia have found both. And so I want us to begin this joyous day of their union with the thought that for all who seek, some may find. Truths are eternal and inspiration can come from anywhere, but truth is delivered through the mind of man. I have selected what I regard as one of the oldest truths from a Hindu legend."

> *Long ago all men were divine. But mankind so abused the privilege that God, the God of all gods, decided the divine should be taken away from them. But he had to hide it where man would never find it again.*
>
> *"Let us bury it deep in the earth," suggested one god. God said, "No, man will develop the means to dig until he finds it."*
>
> *"Then let us throw it into the deepest part of the ocean," proposed another god. God said, "Man will one day learn to dive and someday come across it."*
>
> *"Then let it be hidden among the clouds on the highest mountain." God said, "Man will learn to climb that high some day." Then God said, "I have a better idea. Let us hide it where man will never think to look. Inside man himself."*

Calvin gave way to the religious ceremony. It was at that point that my mind wandered to what had been and what might be. Was I on my way home?

"But me, I'm still on the road headin' for another joint. We always did feel the same we just saw it from another point of view, tangled up in blue."

Robert Dillon
Noble prize winner in poetry

• THE END •

AUTHOR BIOGRAPHY

Gregory W. Young grew up in the insulated, middle class town of West Orange, NJ in the 1950's and 60's. He was taught to love America by the parents who won WWII. He adventured in the wilderness that was northwest New Jersey and Pennsylvania during the 1960's, camping and hunting. Summers were spent boating at the Jersey shore until he was fifteen and old enough to start work as a lifeguard. After high school he attended Valley Forge Military Academy for one year. The powder cask of inner city Newark blew up in 1967 when he was a college student at Monmouth College, Illinois. Vietnam was influencing his generation more and more intensely. Those seminal events shaped him and his generation, calling into question all he had been taught about patriotism and moral and ethical codes. He taught high school for one year in Janesville, Wisconsin before returning to NJ where he continued his post college education and obtained his Practitioner of Mortuary Science License. Greg grew several businesses then took a hiatus to race offshore power boats professionally during racing's glory years of the late 1980's. He won many of his 38 offshore races as a "throttleman" and competed in four World Championships. In 1995 he wrote "The High Cost of Dying", a consumer guide to the funeral, published by Prometheus Publications. The book got excellent reviews and resulted in a consulting gig to ABC Networks "20/20". Along the way he has been a collegiate swimmer, Eagle Scout, front man for bands, lifeguard, ice hockey player and coach, boat builder, public office holder, book store owner, hunter, triathlon swimmer at age 67, and all around raconteur. More successful at some things then others, he is likely to try anything. Today Greg splits his time between Point Pleasant, New Jersey and Sarasota, Florida. Much of his time is spent counseling grieving families and providing repatriation services for those from a foreign country who die in the U.S. .

Made in the USA
Columbia, SC
11 September 2018